HOW TO MAKE A
LIVING IN PARADISE
Southeast Asia Edition

IMPETUS IMPRINT

HOW TO MAKE A LIVING IN PARADISE
Southeast Asia Edition

First Edition © Philip Wylie 2010

Published by Fast Track Publishing, Thailand
E-mail: fasttrackpublishing@gmail.com
Website: www.fasttrackpublishing.com
Fax (Hong Kong): +852-3010-9769

ISBN: 978-616-90336-1-5

BIC Subject Categories:

1FM (Southeast Asia); VSW (Living and working abroad); WTD (Travel tips and advice)

All rights reserved. No part of this publication may be reprinted or reproduced, stored in a retrieval system, or transmitted in any form or by any means, mechanical, electronic, photocopying, recording, or otherwise, without prior permission in writing from the publisher.

Disclaimer: Although the author has been diligent in his research of this book, readers are advised to double-check information before acting upon it. The author and the publishers cannot accept liability for any losses or damages resulting from the guidance contained in this book.

Designed and printed in Thailand

ACKNOWLEDGMENTS

The author wishes to thank all the expats and experts who contributed to this publication, and especially the following people:

Alan Hall, for guidance about investments and financial consultancy

Andrew Bond, for information about website development and search engine optimization

Kevin Bradley and **Brett Evan Lessing,** for their creative input at the gazebo

Les Elliott and **Samantha Burman,** for sharing their knowledge about teaching English in Southeast Asia

Paiboon Publishing, for permission to reproduce text from *How to Establish a Successful Business in Thailand*

Laurie Simmons, for his guidance about online trading with Ebay.com

Sunbelt Asia, for training and employing me as a business manager, broker and advisor

Tommy Schultz, for the photographs on the cover

CONTENTS

PREFACE   9

INTRODUCTION   11

CHAPTER 1: PREPARATION   17

Introduction, 11; Where Is Paradise, 18; Passports, 21; Visas, 22; Health, 24; Culture & Customs, 26; Money Matters, 27; Insurance, 30; Your Cost Of Living, 36; Prohibited Businesses & Occupations, 38; What To Pack In Your Bags, 38

CHAPTER 2: KEYS TO SURVIVAL   41

Introduction, 41; Adjusting To A New Economy, 42; Money Matters, 43; Transportation, 43; Working With The System, 44;Tipping & Negotiating Discounts, 45; Transferring Money Abroad, 45; Local Contacts & Representatives, 46; Support Groups & Networks, 47; Beware The Common Pitfalls, 47; Summary Of Do's & Don'ts, 49

CHAPTER 3: BUYING AN INDEPENDENT BUSINESS   51

Start-Up Vs Buying An Existing Business, 51; Using Business Brokers, 52; Premises: Rent Or Buy, 58; Business Location, 59; Business Development, 60; Type Of Business, 61; Do You Need A Work Permit, 62; Establishing An Investment Budget, 63; Timing – The Best Time To Start, 63; How To Evaluate Businesses, 65; Total Investment, 68; Business Valuation Methods, 69; Adjustment Of Net Annual Profits, 74; Lease Terms, 78; Location, 81; The Seller, 82; Morale, 83; Asset Sale, 83; The Reason For Sale, 85; Due Diligence, 87; The Business Evaluation Checklist, 89; Property Prices, 92; The Stages Of Buying A Business, 93; Sourcing Businesses, 94; Looking For Suitable Premises, 95; How To Deal With Sellers, 97; The Offer To Purchase, 98; Offer To Purchase Checklist, 101; Completion, 102; Recruiting Staff, 104; Preventing Theft, 104

CHAPTER 4: BUYING A FRANCHISE   109

Introduction, 109; Are You A Suitable Franchisee, 109; Franchise Evaluation Checklist, 111; The Advantages & Disadvantages Of Buying A Franchise, 115; Franchise Categories, 119; Contents Of The Operations Manual, 121; Case Study, 122; Further Information, 123

CHAPTER 5: WORKING FREELANCE 125

The Investment, 126; The Office, 127; Website & Email Address, 127; Networking, 128; Promotion, 129; Advertising, 131; Offshore Customers, 132; Administration, 133; Case Studies, 133

CHAPTER 6: ALTERNATIVE APPROACHES 135

Seeking Suitable Investors, 136; Seeking A Suitable Employer, 137; Seeking Sponsorship For Your Project, 138; House-Sitting, 140; Christian Organizations, 140

CHAPTER 7: POPULAR WAYS TO EARN A LIVING 141

Employment With An International Or Foreign-Owned Company, 142; Teaching English, 142; Owning A Local Tourist-Oriented Business, 155; Real Estate & Business Brokering, 155; Property Development & Management, 158; Online Trading & Auctions, 160; Freelance Consulting Of Specialist Services, 163; Writing & Publishing, 164; Volunteering, 168; Website Development, 170; Import/Export & Manufacturing, 179; Online Day Trading Of The Financial Markets, 181

SOUTHEAST ASIA DIRECTORY 183

Brunei	185
Cambodia	187
East Timor	196
Indonesia	198
Laos	204
Malaysia	212
Myanmar	221
Philippines	223
Singapore	236
Thailand	249
Vietnam	260

GLOSSARY OF TERMS 262

ABOUT THE AUTHOR 263

PREFACE

If you are thinking of leaving your home country to live in paradise to improve the quality of your life, this book is for you. Over 6 million of America's best citizens are already thriving overseas. A common regret of expats is that they didn't leave their home country earlier. The biggest obstacle to their freedom is fear which is usually misconceived.

This book has been written by seasoned expats and travelers who are thriving in Southeast Asia. The tips and guidance will save you thousands of dollars and many hours of your time. The author will guide you through established ways of successfully supporting your chosen lifestyle anywhere in Southeast Asia.

This book prepares you for the big escape - and change of lifestyle - by guiding you through the practicalities of passports and visas, health issues and money matters. The book is full of guidance on how to survive in a foreign country and earn a good living doing what you enjoy.

The process of buying an independent business or a franchise is explained. If you have specialized skills and a penchant for networking you must read the chapter about working freelance. There is even a section dedicated to creative pioneers about alternative approaches to making a living and cutting domestic expenditure.

The 12 most popular ways to earn a living in paradise – which are explained in chapter 7 – are: employment with an international or foreign-owned company; teaching English as a foreign language; owning a local tourist-oriented business; real estate and business brokering; property development and management; online trading and auctions; freelance consulting of specialist services; writing and publishing; volunteering; website development; import/export and manufacturing; online day trading of the financial markets.

There are unlimited opportunities for resourceful people to make a living in Southeast Asia. There are lots of teaching opportunities in Southeast Asia, particularly in Thailand, Singapore, Malaysia and Vietnam; work with NGO's in Indonesia, Myanmar and Laos; while adventurous business pioneers are being attracted to Cambodia and Vietnam.

This guide book will help you transform your dream into reality.

Good luck in your honorable quest for freedom and fulfillment! And if you have any questions, do drop me a line. My email address is Philip@philipwylie.com.

Philip Wylie

Chiang Mai
January 2010

INTRODUCTION

Many expats enjoying life in paradise regret not relocating earlier, so don't waste time! Decide what you want to do - and do it! Most successful expats stress the importance of sound preparation and research before relocating overseas. This book has been written to enable a smooth transition for escape artists the world over. This book will save you thousands of dollars, many hours of your time, and headaches too.

HSBC Quality of Life Survey

The Expat Explorer survey was commissioned by HSBC Bank International and conducted by the market research company Freshminds between February and April 2009. The purpose of the survey was to measure the quality of life of surveyed expats in each of 26 geographical locations according to a range of criteria which includes accommodation, healthcare and making friends.

Thailand had an overall ranking of third out of 26 countries for quality of life, followed by Singapore in fourth place (and Hong Kong and Malaysia in 10th and 11th place respectively). The only expat locations to beat Thailand for quality of life were Canada, which came first, and Australia, which came second. Overall, the UK ranked near the bottom in 23rd place.

HSBC Bank International's *Expat Explorer* survey concludes that Hong Kong and India based expats have the highest salaries in the world, with nearly half earning over US$120,000 p.a. But overall Singapore is ranked the top country in the world for earnings, savings, luxury and accommodation, while the UK ranked bottom.

Breaking Down The Wall of Fear

You want to make a massive lifestyle change but your friends and family say you are crazy. Why give up a perfectly good life? Of course it would be difficult to get on the career and property "ladder" again. The media constantly warns us about political instability, terrorism, health issues and safety concerns in those disorganized "undeveloped" nations. How will you support your new life in paradise?

The truth is that most of the above fears are based upon myth. Many people relocate to the tropics, where healthcare is incredibly cheap, to improve their health. In Thailand, for example, it is as safe, or safer, than most places in developed countries. Most expats enjoy a much superior quality of life than their compatriots living in America or Europe. In this book you will find answers to your concerns about how to survive in your chosen destination.

Quality of Life

The main benefit of living overseas is enhanced quality of life. Many expats do not need to get involved with routine domestic chores such as cooking, washing clothes and cleaning because local domestic services are affordable. Most expatriate businesspeople do not require much time to commute to the work. The result is more quality time for leisure and creative pursuits.

Having more time available is beneficial when used appropriately. It suits disciplined writers, artists, researchers and creative people. Moving overseas may facilitate career changers and people experiencing crisis or stress. Retirees living on a limited income will enjoy an enhanced standard of living in many overseas nations. The happiest expats tend to enjoy blending into the local culture and keeping actively involved in healthy activities and projects.

Who This Book Is For?

This book is for anyone considering or planning a new life in Southeast Asia. The enclosed step-by-step roadmap to freedom will be of particular benefit to anyone on a budget or looking for ideas to earn a living overseas. This book also provides valuable information for businesspeople, volunteers, retirees, artists and adventurers.

Inside the following pages you will find lists of golden rules for escape artists and ways to maximize your chances of making a good living in paradise. In the chapter *"Preparation,"* we reveal the most effective ways to prepare for relocation. The chapter covers money matters, visas and passports, inoculations, cultural adjustment and the research you need to do to "land on the ground running".

Some tips in this book are so critically important, they are highlighted in bold. This publication will potentially save you thousands of dollars, many hours of your time and numerous headaches too.

Where is Paradise?

The guidance in this book applies to wherever you call "paradise". It is assumed that the economy in your paradise is weak compared to your home country, which means that your home currency will buy much more.

The question, *"Where is the most beneficial place to stay?"* is examined in chapter 1.

Your 4 Key Options

Unless you have sufficient investment income, or a pension to live on, you have 4 main options to make a good living in paradise. Your options are:

- Employment, including teaching English
- Buying an established business or franchise
- Working freelance using your skills
- Alternative Approaches

Teaching English is a practical way of starting out overseas because schools all over the world are desperately looking for native-American and English speakers to teach. You can learn the local language and research other opportunities while earning a living as a teacher.

Buying an existing business or franchise, requires some investment capital, typically US$3,000 to US$250,000. Chapter 3 explains about investment budgets, how to source suitable businesses for sale, business evaluation, how to buy the business and how to check out the business seller's financials. I highlight the usual pitfalls of buying an existing business and how to avoid them.

Working freelance, which is covered in Chapter 5, usually demands more time and skills than money. Knowledge and networking skills are all-important. Some freelancers invest nothing more than in a box of business (name) cards and a SIM card for their mobile phone. Most freelancers meet their clients in Cafés and restaurants, so no office is necessary. This type of business can be truly mobile.

Alternative approaches to earning a living are limited only by your creativity and motivation. These options are examined in Chapter 6. If you have a sound business idea, why not conduct some research and draft a business plan to present to potential investors? In paradise there are many retirees with pots of money they don't know what to do with! Present your idea at a local expats' club and you may find yourself running a business without needing to invest any money.

The twelve most popular ways for expats to make a living in paradise are included in Chapter 7. Each avenue is summarized, and annexed with sources of further information wherever possible.

Disclaimer

Although the author has been diligent in his research of this book, readers are advised to double-check information before acting upon it. The author and the publishers cannot accept liability for any losses or damages resulting from the guidance contained in this book.

Good Luck!

We hope you enjoy this book and benefit from the information it offers. Don't forget there are over 6 million of the best Americans living overseas and thriving in many ways. When you leave your home country you will enrich your life, learn about new cultures, make new friends and have amazing adventures. If anything goes wrong, or you don't enjoy the experience, you can always go back home, if necessary!

Good luck with your adventure!

CHAPTER 1: PREPARATION

RECONNAISSANCE

Many escapees take an initial reconnaissance trip to their favored destination before actually relocating. This strategy allows you to plan your escape with minimal risk before making any major life decisions. A 2 – 3 week trip may be long enough to establish contacts, arrange long-term accommodation and investigate local work or business opportunities.

The main advantages of a reconnaissance trip to paradise are listed below:

- Avoid quitting your job or business before you have the confidence to turn your dreams into reality
- Identify what you need to take to "paradise" when you finally leave
- Establish a monthly budget for your living expenses
- View rooms and apartments available for rent (on a monthly basis) and collect contact details of suitable landlords
- Meet the local expatriates and learn about visas, work permits, work and business opportunities
- Identify products for sale locally which would sell for a good profit in your home country (to finance the trip)
- Estimate how much money you will need until you support yourself in paradise
- Arrange for a sponsorship letter from a suitable organization to enable you to apply for a one year business visa (if appropriate)
- Make some friends and enjoy your holiday!

The main disadvantage of the reconnaissance trip is the initial additional cost.

Preparation

Research the countries you are most interested in, and plan your itinerary. Read about the culture and customs of the countries you will visit.

Store your possessions with friends or relatives and arrange a mailing address. Throw away your junk and sell or give away whatever you don't need. Avoid spending money on storage because the service is expensive. If you own your home, find a reliable property management agent to take care of it and bank the rental income into your bank account; otherwise instruct your real estate agent to sell your home.

Cancel all unnecessary standing orders and direct debits which are no longer required. Axe all recurring expenses unless absolutely essential. For example, cancel your subscription to your local dvd club. Free yourself of all financial limitations!

WHERE IS PARADISE?

Your idea of paradise is probably different from mine. Your paradise depends you're your values and priorities. Your choice of destination depends upon many factors such as climate, work, business and educational opportunities, exchange rates, political stability, level of crime, language issues, expat community, state of the country's development and environmental factors.

Your choice of destination also depends on visas and immigration policy. Some countries are more receptive to foreign immigrants than others. Foreign policies are continuously changing.

Social Life

Do you need an expat social life or can you blend into the local culture and easily adjust to a completely different lifestyle? Some countries such as Singapore and Thailand have a large expat population offering unlimited luxuries and social activities for expatriate night owls and socialites. Other countries such as Myanmar, which are less developed, have a smaller expat community.

Singapore and Thailand each offer limitless social networking opportunities. Most of the major cities in Southeast Asia offer expat clubs and networks. For a list of social clubs, refer to the *Southeast Asia Directory*.

Climate

If you are sensitive to climatic conditions you should research the weather in your preferred country. Worldwide climate charts are available on the internet (**www.climate-charts.com**). Consider whether you need to bear the additional cost of air-conditioning, or will electric fans suffice?

Cost of Living

Despite the weakening of the dollar, many countries are considerably cheaper to live in than America. Part of your homework is to estimate your monthly cost of living in your preferred country. Cost of living surveys are published by Mercer Human Resource Consulting.(**www.mercerhr.com/costofliving**). If money is not a limiting factor, focus on locations offering the best quality of life. Mercer Human Resource Consulting also publish the *Worldwide Quality of Living Survey*.

Can you live without Starbucks and McDonalds? If not, you need a much higher income. A local cup of coffee may cost one quarter of what Starbucks charge. Similarly a nutritious local meal usually costs a small fraction of what McDonalds charge.

Economy

If you want to own a business overseas, your success will be influenced by the local economy unless you sell to overseas markets. Many expats living overseas own guesthouses and hotels, bars, restaurants, cafes, mini-marts and internet cafés. These businesses are usually dependent on tourism, which is sensitive to news about terrorist activities, crime or disease. Businesses in tourist locations need to make enough profit during the peak season to survive the quieter periods.

Employment

If you need to work there are many opportunities to teach English around the globe. Schools in some countries, such as Japan, Taiwan and South Korea, enable teachers to save money, though there are fewer opportunities in Southeast Asia. However, these same countries have a high cost of living so part-time work is not usually an option. Some expats save enough money for a 6 month holiday after completing their twelve month teaching contract.

For more information about teaching English as a foreign language, refer to Chapter 7 *(Popular Ways To Earn A Living)*.

Health & Safety

Health and safety is another important factor which varies between countries. Ensure you are protected against any prevalent diseases wherever you stay. Relevant information is available on websites for expats and travelers, and at the Centers for Disease Control and Prevention (**www.cdc.gov**).

PASSPORTS

Even if your trip overseas is for just 2 weeks, ensure your passport is valid for at least another 6 months. Many countries do not allow foreign visitors if their passports are valid for less than 6 months. Passports can be renewed for a further 10 years in your home country, or at your local embassy in paradise.

Ensure you have enough unused blank pages in your passport in case you need to take regular border crossings to comply with immigration policy. Pages in your passport fill up quickly with visas and stamps by immigration officers in each country of your itinerary.

It is advisable to record contact information of your next of kin in, or with, your passport. In many countries foreigners are recommended to register their arrival with their local embassy or consulate.

Always keep your passport in a secure place, and a copy of your passport in your wallet. If you lose your passport, notify your local embassy or consulate as soon as possible. Usually it is necessary to deposit your passport with motor vehicle hirers until you return the vehicle and pay the hire fees. Sometimes hotels and guesthouses hold passports of their customers.

VISAS

It is essential to have a valid visa at all times for any foreign trip or residence. Even if you have a 12 month visa, you may have to leave the country every 90 days or "check in" at the local immigration office periodically. Failure to comply with immigration regulations can result in fines and even imprisonment.

Part of your preparatory homework is researching the visa requirements (and options) for your country of destination. Visa information is available at consulates and embassies (for the country of destination) in your home country. Most consulates and embassies provide visa information on their own websites. Additionally there are many independent online travel websites offering forums specifically for travelers and expatriates.

Typical visa classifications are Tourist, Business, Marriage and Retirement. Visas are either "single-entry" or "multiple-entry" for the duration of the document. The single-entry visa expires when the holder leaves the country, whereas the multiple-entry visa is valid for the entire term. Some visas offer a choice of durations (typically 3 months, 6 months or 12 months).

PREPARATION

Visa application forms can be obtained from local embassies and consulates. Also the forms can usually be downloaded from the embassy's website.

Identify the most suitable embassy or consulate using either of the following websites: **www.embassyinformation.com** and **www.embassyworld.com**. Be aware that consulates and embassies often have different policies for issuance of visas in each country. Consulates tend to offer more favorable terms to visa applicants than embassies. Phone the embassy or consulate immediately before making the visa application to check that the terms and conditions of application have not changed.

Business or "non-immigrant" visas may enable residence in paradise for 3 months, 12 months or longer. The visa application may require an accompanying sponsorship letter by an appropriate local organization. Be aware that most immigration officers prefer to issue visas to smartly dressed professionals, students or businesspeople rather than scruffy hippies.

Business visas do not usually entitle holders to work. Foreign workers need to apply for a work permit. Usually business visas are a prerequisite for obtaining a work permit. Business visas can be used without work permits for research and investment.

If your journey is less than 4 weeks in duration you may be able to obtain a visa on arrival. Otherwise apply for a tourist visa (if appropriate) at the local consulate or embassy.

All visas applications require accompanying passport photographs, a completed application form and fee. Business or non-immigrant visas usually require additional documentation such as resumé and letter of invitation by a local sponsor.

Never "overstay" your visa unless unavoidable. If it is not possible to extend your visa at the local immigration office, you must leave the country before the visa expires and apply for a new one in another country.

HEALTH

If you register with a local hospital, keep a copy of your hospital registration card in your wallet always.

Information about health precautions and inoculations for each country is available at the Centers for Disease Control & Prevention (CDC) website: **www.cdc.gov**. Before leaving, ensure you have inoculated yourself for all potential diseases in the countries you intend to travel to.

Keep a record of all your inoculations with dates. Note when it is necessary to renew your inoculations.

Eye Care

If you wear contact lenses, keep a supply of spare lenses and a record of the specifications of your lenses. Pack a pair of spectacles in your luggage.

In Vietnam, where there is high humidity and air pollution, travelers are prone to conjunctivitis or other bacterial infection of the eye. Do not wear contact lenses if you catch an eye infection.

Malaria and Dengue Fever

Currently there is no antidote for malaria and dengue fever. If you plan to travel in places where the risk of contracting these diseases is high, do take precautions to avoid being bitten by mosquitoes.

Dengue Fever and its potentially fatal variant, Dengue Haemorrhagic Fever (DHF), affect hundreds of people around the world. However, dengue fever can be avoided.

Both malaria and dengue fever is transmitted by mosquitoes. Aedes Aegypti is the mosquito which causes dengue fever.

Symptoms of dengue fever include pain in the bones accompanied by high temperature. After 7 days of incubation, fever and headaches (behind the eyes) begin. The fever is also known as "Break Bone Fever" due to the acute muscle pains which patients experience.

Prevention of dengue fever begins at home. Ensure there is no stagnant water within a radius of quarter of a kilometer of your home. Common breeding grounds for mosquitoes include used car tires, saucers under pot plants and water tanks.

Other precautions include wearing long trousers and long-sleeved shirts. Apply mosquito repellent to exposed parts of your body. **Ensure that your mosquito repellent contains DEET.**

The most effective ways of preventing malaria are to use mosquito repellant containing DEET on exposed skin, sleeping under a mosquito net impregnated with Permethrin, using mosquito coils and wearing long clothes.

Medication for malaria tends to be expensive and ineffective. Chloroquine and Paludrine, which causes nausea, relieves the symptoms of malaria but does not prevent the disease.

If you contract malaria, aim to check into a malaria clinic within 24 hours of developing the fever. If you decide to use medication, Malarone is the most effective drug.

CULTURE & CUSTOMS

Research the local culture and customs before you leave. ***Culture Shock!*** Publications provide cultural guides for each country.

The general rule for expats is to respect the local culture, customs, religion and monarchy. Always dress appropriately, particularly at government offices and places of worship. Never behave aggressively with locals and settle any disputes immediately if possible. Remember that we are allowed to stay in paradise as guests.

Learn about the laws of your host country and keep out of trouble. Expats are best advised to blend into the culture instead of attracting unnecessary attention.

MONEY MATTERS

Objective

Minimize your monthly expenditure and cancel all financial commitments unless they support your plan to relocate abroad.

Emergency Cash

It is advisable to carry with you some emergency cash with you at all times. Do not use this money unless you need to settle a dispute on the spot. A small cash settlement may enable you to avoid legal disputes, physical danger, police custody and even imprisonment.

Secure your Cash

If you plan to travel in a relatively dangerous area, divide up your cash and valuables and keep them in different parts of your clothing and luggage. Buy a second cheap wallet and fill with a small amount of cash to throw away in the event of a possible mugging.

Travelers' Checks

Buy some travelers' checks in either dollars or euros and keep a separate record of the check numbers in case you loose them. You can apply for a refund if the checks are lost or stolen. Travelers' checks are a useful backup in case you cannot use credit cards or ATMs. Some countries, such as Loas, have few ATMs.

Exchange rates for cashing traveler's checks are usually favorable compared to bank notes or withdrawing cash from the ATM.

Buy enough travelers' checks to enable you to buy a flight ticket back home if necessary.

Online Banking

Keep control of your finances. Open an online banking account so you can manage your money from anywhere in the world. Keep your online security details, including password, secure at all times. Avoid the possibility of fraud and never respond to any emails requesting your online security details.

Bank Charges & Interest

If possible, pay off all your loans and overdrafts before moving overseas to avoid the expense of bank interest. Keep your bank account in credit always. Cancel all unnecessary standing orders and direct debits. Maximize your bank interest receivable on your savings by switching accounts as required. Arrange a direct debit to settle your credit card balance each month.

Taxes

A U.S citizen or resident alien is generally subject to U.S. tax on total worldwide income. However many countries have double taxation treaties with USA, enabling Americans living in those countries to benefit from a tax credit for any taxes paid overseas.

Further information about filing tax returns with the IRS is provided on their website (**www.irs.gov/faqs/**). The international tax law telephone hotline number is +1 (215) 516 2000.

The IRS website (**www.irs.gov**) explains how to file your tax return electronically from another country.

For information about tax exclusions for Americans residing overseas, refer to the following IRS webpage: www.irs.gov/publications/p54/index.html. American citizens who are working legally (and subject to personal taxes) abroad can earn up to US$91,400 (in 2009) without liability to U.S taxation. It is necessary to remain outside USA for at least 12 months and to spend a maximum of 29 days in USA each year to be eligible for these tax exclusions.

Social Security

U.S. Treasury Department regulations prohibit sending payments to you if you are in Cuba or North Korea. If you are a U.S. citizen and are in Cuba or North Korea, you can receive all of your payments that were withheld once you leave that country and go to another country where payments can be sent.

Social Security restrictions prohibit sending payments to individuals in Cambodia and Vietnam. Generally, you cannot receive payments while you are in one of the aforementioned countries nor can payments be sent to someone on your behalf. However, there are possible exceptions for certain eligible beneficiaries in countries other than Cuba or North Korea.

To qualify for an exception, you must agree to the conditions of payment. One of the conditions is that you must appear in person at the U.S. Embassy each month to receive your benefits. Contact your nearest U. S. Social Security office or U.S. Embassy or consulate for additional information about these conditions and whether you might qualify for an exception.

For further information about social security, refer to the U.S. Government's website at **www.ssa.gov/pgm/formspubs.htm**.

Wills

A will is a legal document declaring who you want to benefit from your estate when you die. The document must be signed, dated and witnessed.

If you plan to transfer money or assets overseas you should write a will and keep a signed copy with your lawyer and next of kin. A separate will should be prepared for each country of residence.

INSURANCE

Introduction

Insurance is a financial product which offers peace of mind for people worried about the unexpected costs arising from accidents, robberies, sickness and other disasters. Insurance is no substitute for preventing disease, driving carefully or securing your personal belongings.

Your insurance requirements depend on your ability to pay unexpected bills, your age, state of health and lifestyle, the value of your personal property and the risk of crime, accidents and disease in the country you are visiting.

The most common problems involving insurance claims are vehicle accidents, malaria or dengue fever and loss or theft of property. Many "developing" countries are safer than parts of America and Europe.

Insurance policies contain exclusions, thresholds and excesses (or deductions). Exclusions are items which are not insured. The Threshold indicates the maximum amount of the claim for each classification under the policy. The excess is the amount deducted from each item claimed. The policy premium increases if the policy has a lower excess.

Book an insurance policy with a reputable company. Some insurance companies have a reputation for paying out a small percentage of claims after months of correspondence. Other companies have a reputation for settling insurance claims in full, quickly and without any fuss.

Travel Insurance

Travel insurance is a multipurpose financial product for a specified term. Many travel insurance products are designed for overseas holidays of up to 12 months in duration. It is not possible to claim on travel insurance policies after relocating abroad. In the event of a travel insurance claim, the insurer may ask for evidence that you are not permanently residing overseas. For example they may ask for a copy of your return flight ticket and passport. Apply for special expatriate insurance when you officially reside overseas.

Be aware that in many countries motorcycles and cars are rented without any insurance. This means that if you have an accident you may have to pay for repairs and medical costs even if it is not your fault. If your hired motorcycle is stolen, you would have to buy a replacement. Therefore check that your travel or expatriate insurance policy covers these potential losses.

Travel insurance policies typically cover medical expenses relating to accidents and sickness, replacement cost of personal property if lost or stolen, costs incurred in the event of death, loss of passport, or delay or cancellation of any flights booked and paid for. Be aware that even though the cost of hospitalization may be one tenth of that charged in USA, the expense could still exceed US$1,000.

Travel insurance is valid only for the period of your holiday or the term of the policy (if it lapses before you return home). The insurer may pay for medical treatment while you are staying overseas, but not after you return home.

Travel insurance policies usually provide benefits in the event of flight cancellation or delays. If a flight is cancelled, the airline is responsible for your alternative travel arrangements which may include hotel accommodation. If possible, use the same airline if you have connecting flights so your airline will book you on their next flight at no additional cost. Always allow at least 3 hours between estimated time of arrival and departure time of your connecting flights. Some airlines and online travel agents offer optional flight insurance.

If you are traveling overseas for the first time on a reconnaissance trip of up to 3 months, you are strongly recommended to take out travel insurance.

Expat Insurance

Unfortunately there is no multipurpose insurance policy for expats covering medical expenses, home contents, life, and motor vehicle. Most expats take out medical insurance policies which are specifically designed for people who live overseas.

If you have dependents you should consider an offshore life insurance policy or term insurance. Term insurance is a composite health and life insurance policy for a defined period (usually one year).

Many of the most reputable expat insurers are based in UK. The need for medical insurance – and the cost - increases with age of the insured person.

Step 1: Identify the Insurance You Already Have

Many travelers and expats waste money by doubly insuring themselves. Whilst taking out more insurance than necessary may provide extra peace of mind, it is an additional drain on your finances.

The major credit card companies insure all products and services purchased using their payment system. Therefore, book any flight tickets and valuables using a credit card such as Visa. If your flight is cancelled you can claim a refund from the airline or your credit card provider.

Whether you buy or rent a vehicle, ensure you have a motor insurance policy covering medical expenses in the event of an accident. I have successfully claimed all hospital expenses on my motorcycle policy in Thailand and the annual premium cost less than US$20.

If you work overseas, your employer should provide health insurance as part of your remuneration package.

If you travel with your computer notebook maybe you already have worldwide insurance cover for loss, theft and repairs. If so, keep a copy of your insurance policy with you. Scan the policy and keep an electronic copy.

Citizens of the European Union may be entitled to free medical treatment under the National Health Scheme. Therefore some expats from Europe may choose to return to their home country to receive free medical treatment if they get chronically sick.

Step 2: Establish Your Insurance Needs

Even though medical bills may be a small fraction of the cost in America, an operation in paradise can still cost US$1,000+. Accidents and disease can strike us at any time. Your decision about insurance depends on your ability to pay unexpected bills, your age and state of health, and your perceived risk of injury, accident or robbery.

If you drive a motor vehicle overseas ensure the vehicle is insured. If you travel where there is a high risk of malaria, protect yourself from mosquitoes. Avoid traveling with valuables if possible. Keep your passport and valuable items in a safe place such as a safe deposit box.

Step 3: Identify Appropriate Insurance Policies

Look for an insurance policy with a reputable company which fills the gap in your insurance needs.

Beware! There is no insurance policy covering loss or theft of data stored on your computer or mobile phone. So take regular backups of important data onto an external drive or on paper. Remember that no insurance claim will fully compensate your loss of any sentimental photographs or gifts from family or special friends.

Your choice of insurance policy depends upon many factors. If you have sufficient savings to cover all possible problems you may even decide to forgo the expense of insurance.

How To Make An Insurance Claim

If you are involved in an accident or robbery and you want to file an insurance claim, obtain a written report from the local police station as soon as possible. It may be necessary to attend the police station with a local representative unless your language skills are up to par.

You will need to complete the insurer's claim form, which may be downloadable from the internet. Usually the insurer will require the original purchase invoice for the property lost or stolen or other evidence of its value and your ownership.

Small claims of under US$100 may not be worth the time and inconvenience. The cost of your claim may include return travel to a local police station, photocopying, postage and phone calls. The claim may be settled after several months' correspondence and follow-up telephone calls from overseas. Finally, remember that insurance policies do not offer any compensation for the time involved managing the claim.

Other Tips

- If you buy your own vehicle, consider comprehensive insurance (which covers damage and theft of your vehicle)

- Consider an inexpensive local accident insurance policy

- For health insurance, check out the local BUPA medical insurance, Healthcare International (www.healthcareinternational.com) and others

- Consult a professional independent financial consultant specializing in expatriate wealth management

YOUR COST OF LIVING

When you relocate, your cost of living will plummet hopefully. It is useful to estimate your revised cost of living so you are aware of any deficit which needs to be offset by earnings.

The main costs to include in your budget are:

- Accommodation (and services)
- Food & drink
- Telephone calls and internet access
- Passport and visa administration
- Travel (including border crossings to meet visa regulations)
- Insurance premiums
- Consumables, clothing and healthcare
- Entertainment

PREPARATION

Add any costs incurred in your home country such as bank charges, storage costs or annual membership fees of clubs or associations. Subtract any interest received on your savings accounts and any other investment income.

Your cost of living depends on your lifestyle. Estimate your monthly cost of living by referring to standard wage rates of expats (such as English teachers) in your country of choice. For information about teaching English abroad, refer to **www.daveseslcafe.com**.

Standard accommodation costs in Chiang Mai, Thailand, are US$60 per month for a basic room with separate bathroom, US$190 per month for a one bedroom condominium, and US$600 per month for a 4 bedroom house. Search for houses or apartments for rent in your chosen location using an internet search engine to research accommodation costs.

Your cost of food and drink depends upon whether you eat local or Western food in restaurants, or whether you cook your own food. Local food is usually much cheaper than international cuisine. Don't expect to save much money by cooking your own meals unless you have sufficient people to share the cost with.

You may choose to buy or rent a motorcycle or car. Ensure that your vehicle is properly insured. In many countries, motor insurance just covers medical expenses in the event of an accident. Consider applying for a local driving license if you plan to stay.

There are many places where escapees can enjoy a good quality of life on under US$1,000 per month. Cost of living is higher in locations which are more "developed" or fashionable. You can live extremely cheaply if you can quickly adjust to the local lifestyle and avoid McDonalds.

PROHIBITED BUSINESSES & OCCUPATIONS

Some countries protect their domestic economy by prohibiting foreigners from engaging in specified businesses and occupations. Before starting a business or working freelance, check the country's laws pertaining to prohibited businesses and occupations for aliens.

WHAT TO PACK IN YOUR BAGS

Always carry some form of ID with you. Keep a photocopy of your passport in your wallet at all times. It is also useful to keep either a local driving license or an international driving license.

Keep your passport (with valid visa) secure always. Keep the document in a safe place – preferably under lock and key – whenever you are not traveling. If you lose your passport it may take your embassy weeks to replace it.

The following is a list of items you should take with you:

- Travel guidebook & other country information
- Travel or expat insurance documents (and keep a copy separately)
- Purchase invoices for any valuable items in your baggage (with a separate copy)

- Spare passport photographs (in your wallet when traveling)
- Mosquito repellent containing DEET and mosquito net (if dengue fever or malaria may be a potential threat)
- Travelers' checks (for emergencies)
- Local currency (if possible)
- Credit card and/or ATM card allowing withdrawals worldwide
- PC flash drive with copies of important documents (eg CV, certificates, references)
- Medical supplies
- Digital camera
- Books and MP3 player
- Combination lock for your baggage and lockers
- Mobile phone
- Computer notebook (if required)

Check the baggage allowance of your airline carrier. This information is provided with your flight ticket. Most airlines allow between 15Kg and 30Kg plus additional hand luggage of around 7Kg. Charges for overweight baggage can be expensive and must be paid at the airline's check-in desk. Avoid paying excess baggage fees if possible.

Don't pack too many clothes if you are traveling to the tropics where clothing is cheap to buy. Use your coveted baggage allowance for items which are difficult to buy or expensive at your destination.

If you wear contact lenses, keep a record of the relevant specifications with you and pack a pair of spectacles.

Information

Keep a backup of all important contact information. Backup all important data onto a computer or memory card whether you keep your contacts in your mobile phone, notebook or address book. Be prepared for the possible loss of your mobile phone, luggage or wallet. Many travelers recommend sending themselves an email with an attached file containing all important contacts, references and scanned certificates.

CHAPTER 2: KEYS TO SURVIVAL

INTRODUCTION

The main purpose of this chapter is to provide tips on how to survive – and thrive – in your chosen destination. The main guidelines are:

- Be disciplined about looking after your health and keep your inoculations up-to-date
- Keep focused on your project, business or other reasons for residing abroad
- Develop relationships with local people and expats and avoid making any enemies
- Keep your activities legal and trouble-free
- Aim to live off your local earnings and transfer money from home only when absolutely necessary; for example, to start a business
- Maintain your interest in the local area by visiting new places, meeting people and developing yourself
- Keep your insurance up-to-date
- Never "overstay" your visa
- Try to integrate into the local culture and make some contribution to the community
- Keep out of trouble and settle any potential disputes immediately without involving the police or lawyers

You have started your new life in paradise. Ideally you do not have any financial commitments or costs in your home country. Hopefully you can withdraw cash anywhere from your savings or checking account using your ATM card. Now your goal is to earn enough money to cover your monthly living costs in paradise.

ADJUSTING TO A NEW ECONOMY

Avoid comparing local prices with equivalent prices back home. Whilst your new cost of living may be much lower, your income will be lower too. Instead of saying *"Wow, everything's so cheap!"* and buying drinks for everyone in sight, save your money and adjust to a new economy as quickly as possible.

Learn the local language as quickly as possible so you can converse with local people. When you speak the local language proficiently you are more likely to be treated as a local. This means you will be able to negotiate higher discounts on the goods you buy. You will also learn more about the local culture and customs.

Rent accommodation by the month instead of paying the daily rate. Long term accommodation rates can be 20% - 50% of the daily room rates. It may be necessary to pay a security deposit and contract to pay metered electricity costs separately.

Eat and drink what the locals eat and drink. You don't have to eat the spiciest papaya salad or insects, but you can save a lot of money by avoiding western menus. Street noodle vendors generally provide much more nutrition than western junk food. If you have spare time, investigate the best deals in town for food, drink and accommodation.

MONEY MATTERS

Insurance

Renew your insurance policy and pay the renewal premium before it expires. Even if you intended to pay your insurer's renewal premium, they will not settle any claim relating to events which happen after the policy expires. So make sure you pay your insurance premiums on time.

Bank Account

Apply for a bank account with a reputable local bank. Usually a personal bank account can be opened by completing an application form, showing your passport and depositing a nominal amount of cash.

TRANSPORTATION

Once you have made the commitment to live abroad for an "extended period" save your money by buying a new or used motorcycle or car. Check the legality of the vehicle. Is it registered and plated? Register the vehicle in your own name if you are allowed to do so. Check the identity of the owner to his or her personal identity card or passport. Keep your vehicle ownership documents in a safe place.

Keep the motor tax and insurance up-to-date for your vehicle. Ensure that the insurance policy covers you for medical expenses in the event of an accident. My motorcycle insurance policy, which cost under US$20 per annum, reimbursed all my hospital costs when I fractured my arm in an accident.

Never be tempted to drive a motorcycle without wearing a safety helmet. Many drivers in developing countries learn their driving skills "on the road" so road safety is a major issue. Of course driving a big motorbike without a helmet feels liberating, but that feeling diminishes after an accident.

I purchased a good quality used 200cc Honda motorbike for under US$1,500. After four years of relatively trouble-free motoring, it is still worth over US$1,000. A similar motorbike would rent for US$12 per day. Buying a vehicle will save you money if you stay overseas for at least a year.

Note that in some developing countries, vehicle fatalities occur 50 times as often as in USA or UK. If you choose to drive, drive carefully. Many people drive under the influence of alcohol. Many expats complain that if an accident occurs, foreigners are deemed to be at fault regardless of the actual facts.

WORKING WITH THE SYSTEM

One foreigner alone cannot change a system and culture that has developed over thousands of years, so don't try to change it.

Many travelers and expats complain about corruption and bribery by police and Government officials. Maybe the police accept bribes as an alternative to paying a fine at the police station in the event of a traffic offence. Would you pay a small bribe and drive away, or pay a higher fine at the police station?

Remember that the police and government officers earn low salaries in many countries. Gifting and paying commission for business referrals is a common practice in Asia.

TIPPING & NEGOTIATING DISCOUNTS

Tipping is a common practice among backpackers and other holiday makers. Expats and other local residents do not tip so often. Usually owners of small business prefer repeat custom to one-off business, regardless of whether you leave a tip.

Some developing countries operate a two-tier pricing system, one for the local residents and another for the foreigners. Indonesia and Vietnam use this discriminatory pricing system extensively. Expats residing in such countries are sometimes able to buy products at the local rate depending on their language ability, negotiating skills and local relationships.

If you need to buy any expensive items or bulk purchases you should consider asking a local friend to negotiate on your behalf. In the Middle East negotiations tend to benefit anyone willing to socialize for hours while drinking green tea.

TRANSFERRING MONEY ABROAD

Do not transfer money abroad unless absolutely necessary. Live on your local income if possible.

For small cash withdrawals use your ATM card. For larger amounts, the most common method of transfer is by wire transfer using SWIFT or IBAN. The overseas bank will require the account name and number of your local bank account together with the swift code and contact details of the bank. Transfer times vary between 3 and 5 days.

Usually it is advantageous to send the funds in foreign currency for exchange at your correspondent bank in paradise; this way you are likely to receive a better rate of exchange. If you are remitting funds to a local company, provide your bank with the company name as a reference, such as "Investment in ABC Ltd."

Ask your correspondent bank for a foreign exchange form within 4 weeks of the money transfer. Keep this document safely in case you want to repatriate the funds free of withholding tax in the future.

LOCAL CONTACTS & REPRESENTATIVES

Many expats discover that local relationships are more valuable than money in developing countries. Most expats live overseas for enhanced quality of life, though some do so to accumulate capital if they receive a generous expat remuneration package in a "hardship" territory. If your motive for living overseas is to improve the quality of your life, you are probably sacrificing earning potential in return for time to do whatever you please.

If you know an honest local person in a position of authority you have a great advantage. They may act on your behalf in a legal dispute. If you have any influential local friends who work as lawyers, policemen or village leaders, keep their contact details on you at all times. You never you when you may need their help. Contacts of this kind are more valuable than any insurance policy.

SUPPORT GROUPS & NETWORKS

The first line of support for every expat in danger is their local embassy or consulate. Refer to the websites at www.embassyworld.com and www.embassyinformation.com to locate your nearest embassy or consulate.

Most popular expat locations offer expat clubs and special interest groups as well as Chambers of Commerce and other organizations listed in Chapter 5 (*Working Freelance*). An international directory of Chambers of Commerce is available at: www.worldchambers.com. There are social support groups and clubs, such as The Hash Hound Harriers (www.gthhh.com), dotted around the globe.

Many countries offer local support groups for codependents with Codependents Anonymous (www.codependents.org). Support for alcoholics is offered by Alcoholics Anonymous (www.alcoholics-anonymous.org).

BEWARE THE COMMON PITFALLS

The common pitfalls experienced by expats are not taking care of their health and not keeping occupied in projects or hobbies.

A common issue for expats is falling into bad habits such as regular drinking at local bars and temptations of the flesh. There are probably more recreational opportunities in paradise and it requires self-discipline not to lose yourself and your purpose.

Even if you plan to retire overseas, you may benefit mentally by volunteering or teaching, even if you don't need the money. For many expats, boredom is the greatest curse. Expats usually have more hours to fill if they don't need to do any domestic chores or commute a long distance to work. Why cook food yourself if it's as cheap or cheaper to buy a meal in a restaurant? Why do your own laundry and ironing when the local laundry service costs just US$12 per month?

Some expats make the mistake of buying a bar or other business for their local spouse or partner without properly appraising it. Sometimes they buy the business for a spouse who has no interest in working. The idea of having your own bar as a "hobby" business may seem exciting, but many of part-time businesses fail.

Another common mistake is rushing into marriage, buying property and registering it in their spouse's name, and later losing both spouse and property. There are ways of protecting your financial interests and it is advisable to discuss these options with a reputable lawyer.

SUMMARY

DO:

- Try to learn the local language and understand the culture
- Exchange books, music cds and dvds with other expats and travelers
- Avoid any protracted legal disputes by settling issues "on the spot"
- Keep occupied and change your daily routines to avoid stagnation
- Look after your health by keeping fit, eating well and not drinking too much
- Be careful about drugs in countries whether there are severe penalties for even possession
- Safeguard your passport and money always
- Establish a friendship with a reliable and authoritative local representative
- Eat and drink local food and beverages
- If you drive a motorcycle, always wear a safety helmet on the road and apply for a local driving license
- If you have significant assets overseas, ensure your interests are properly protected, and both you and your spouse write a will

DON'T:

- Get angry or aggressive with the local people
- Criticize the country's monarchy or religion
- Attract too much attention to yourself, particularly if you are successful
- Overstay your visa
- Don't invest in a business without conducting adequate due diligence

CHAPTER 3:
BUYING AN INDEPENDENT BUSINESS

START-UP VS BUYING AN EXISTING BUSINESS

If you want to run your own business overseas you can either start up from scratch or buy an existing business (or going concern).

Starting up from Scratch

This option is usually the riskiest, but it allows most potential for independence, reward and personal gratification. Business risk can be limited by thorough research, planning and support by suitable local partners, associates and employees.

The foreigners who usually succeed in start-ups are suitably knowledgeable and experienced in their chosen field of business. They are aware of their strengths and weaknesses, and find others to take responsibility for their areas of weakness. Finally, they are resourceful and totally committed to the success of their business.

Before starting up a new business, you should be acquainted with the local culture and customs, and have a local support network. It may take a few months to find a suitable local partner and premises. After the aforementioned fundamentals are in place, and you have a realistic business plan, maybe you are ready to proceed.

Buying an Existing Business

An existing business is usually purchased as a turnkey operation. Ideally the buyer earns a living from the date of purchase. Working capital (or current assets, such as inventory) is usually included in the purchase price.

Choose a business which generates sufficient profit to support your desired lifestyle. Whether you buy a business via a business broker or direct from the seller, you are responsible for validating the seller's representations, including all financial information provided.

Whenever possible, obtain independent impartial professional advice to evaluate the business.

USING BUSINESS BROKERS

Brokers (or agents) are intermediaries acting on behalf of the business owner (or seller). The broker has a duty of care to the business seller. The seller agrees to pay the broker a commission on completion of the business sale.

Business brokers specialise in the sale of going concerns. Businesses listed by brokers usually employ staff and include fixed assets (including furniture and equipment) and inventory. Typical listings include small to medium sized guest houses, internet cafés, bars, restaurants, hotels, resorts and factories.

You are allowed to register with as many brokers as you please.

Business Listings

Sales turnover of most listings offered by business brokers is under US$250,000 per annum. These listings tend to be priced in the range US$3,000 to US$250,000.

Brokers do not usually guarantee the quality of any businesses they list for sale. The businesses listed may be fundamentally flawed, and it's the buyer's responsibility to identify the problem. Don't expect the broker to spend extra time doing your research, and jeopardizing their fee.

Business Brokers' Fees

The transfer of business ownership is much more complicated than the transfer of property. Businesses usually involve landlords, employees, fixed assets & inventory, customers, training, accounts and financial statements. Business transfer also requires confidentially.

Business brokers charge higher fees than real estate agents because of the additional work involved. Business brokers typically charge between 7% and 12% of purchase price, compared to 3–5% charged by realtors

Although the business seller contracts with the broker to pay the above fees, the buyer ultimately foots this bill. The businesses listed by brokers rarely include genuine bargains. The broker has incentive to sell for the highest price possible.

Where to find the Bargains

Real bargains are found by chance, usually by word of mouth; typically a foreigner leaves the country quickly due to personal circumstances (eg illness, divorce, partnership problems or death in the family). Therefore, bargains do exist but don't wait for a bargain or life may pass you by. Instead conduct due diligence and find the best property for your investment budget.

Checking the Details

It is the buyer's responsibility to check all information provided by the business owner and their broker. Usually, brokers simply pass on information from seller to buyer without checking it. The broker has a responsibility to query the seller's representations only when, in their professional opinion, it does not appear to be correct.

Brokers may assume their client is truthful unless their knowledge and experience leads them to another conclusion. The broker is negligent if he or she knowingly passes on false information to the prospective buyer.

In-house Legal Services

Some business brokers provide an in-house legal service to assist with the drafting of leases or the processing of work permits and licenses. Some brokers rent serviced or virtual offices to their clients.

The downside of using your broker's lawyer would become apparent if your broker negligently sold a business to you, or the lawyer drafted your contract to the advantage of the seller. Who would the lawyer support: their employer or one of many customers?

Buyers are best advised to instruct the services of a neutral (or impartial) lawyer to avoid any conflict of interests.

Preparation

If you want the best possible service from your business broker, act like a serious buyer. Turn up to the appointment on time and look like you mean business. Have answers to the following questions ready:

- What is your budget (or how much are you willing to spend)?
- How much cash do you have available to spend now?
- What businesses are you interested in?
- Where do you want to base your business?

The budget you give the broker should be a proportion (say 75%) of your total investment. Keep to your budget. Allow for all possible additional costs of setup, including prepaid rent, security deposits, legal fees, remodeling costs and replacement of equipment.

Some professional brokers screen buyer to establish that they have funding in place to meet their investment budget. This practise is designed to eliminate "tire kickers", dreamers or people just wanting a free tour of the local businesses for sale. Don't forget that land and property can take years to sell, in case you have no liquid funds available.

Review the broker's business listings via their website before your initial meeting. Note down the references of the businesses you are most interested in. This will enable you and your broker to save time.

The broker will probably ask you to sign a Non-Disclosure Agreement (NDA). Sometimes these documents are referred to as Confidentiality Agreements.

Confidentiality

If the seller's employees discover their employer is selling the business they may lose interest and leave. If customers realise their supplier is for sale, they may switch suppliers. Both possibilities lead to diminishing profits, so confidentiality is critically important in business brokerage.

The NDA is your agreement to keep the seller's information confidential. You may be given access to private financial information. By signing this document you agree not to tell anyone about the sale of the broker's listings without the seller's permission.

The NDA will probably contain a clause stating that all negotiations between buyer and seller are mediated by the broker. If the buyer colludes with the seller to avoid payment of the broker's fees, the buyer may also be liable to pay the fees.

If you refuse to sign this agreement, your broker will probably not show you any businesses for sale. Usually there is nothing onerous to the buyer in this agreement.

Business Viewings

As you review the business, make a mental note of every possible opportunity for developing it. Perhaps you know of appropriate additional product lines, ways of improving the layout, or control systems to install.

If you want your broker to show you more businesses, demonstrate to him or her that the businesses you have viewed are unsuitable. Legitimate reasons include poor location, over-budget, high rent or even distrust of the seller. Put the onus on the broker to show you suitable businesses.

Questions for your Broker

- What is the period of the lease? Your lawyer may be able to negotiate a favourable new lease with the landlord.
- What are the earnings of the business?
- Why is the owner selling? Is the business failing, or is there a legitimate reason for the sale (eg health or partnership problems)?
- How long has the business been on the broker's books?
- Is the agency Sole & Exclusive, or Multiple Agency?

The best business listings tend to be exclusive.

The Advantages of using Brokers

- The service is free to buyers with no obligation to buy
- The broker and lawyer may assist with your research
- The broker's in-house lawyer may answer your legal questions without charge
- The broker should save you time by obtaining information from the seller on your behalf
- You may view many businesses for sale in a short period of time
- A reputable broker will return your deposit if your offer is rejected or your conditions of offer are not fulfilled

The Disadvantages of using Brokers

- The businesses listed are usually optimally priced for the seller

- The broker's fee is factored into the selling price
- The broker's duty of care is to the seller, so the buyer is responsible for validating the seller's financial statements and representations
- The businesses are without any guarantee of quality (unless otherwise indicated)
- You may hear about the listed business from other sources after you sign the NDA with the broker
- The Broker may lock you into using their in-house lawyer (who will probably ask you to sign disclaimers protecting the broker from any professional liability).

PREMISES: RENT OR BUY?

Do you need Business Premises?

If you are a freelance professional you may consider renting a virtual office rather than paying for a full office set-up.

Virtual Offices

Virtual offices suit freelance website designers, internet traders, property developers, graphic designers, editors and computer programmers and other businesses that do not need a "brick & mortar" office.

Most of the above practitioners work from home and save the cost of renting an office. They meet clients in suitable cafés, hotels or restaurants. The keys to their business are mobile phone, computer notebook, website, email and business cards.

Rent or Buy Premises?

Property investment is a specialist business which demands management time and expense. Therefore you are best advised to rent premises initially.

The Advantages of renting Premises

- In many countries rents are low relative to property prices
- Renting allows more cash available for business assets, including inventory and equipment, so you minimise your investment
- Property in developing countries can take a long time to liquidate, sometimes several years
- The landlord is normally responsible for the building, maintenance and repairs
- Foreigners are not allowed to own property in many developing countries

BUSINESS LOCATION

The location of any retail business is critically important. If your business depends upon "passing trade", do not compromise on location. There is intense competition for the most favourable trading locations. Allow at least six months to find suitable premises.

If your business does not rely upon passing trade, spare the expense of a prime business location. For example software development companies and factories are usually based on the outskirts of major cities.

BUSINESS DEVELOPMENT

Do you want to develop an existing business which needs improvement? Or would you prefer to pay a higher price for a fully "optimized" business with minimal scope for improvement? Development demands creativity backed by management ability and application. Do you really have the resourcefulness to transform a fledging business?

Let us consider three levels of business development: the undeveloped business, the semi-developed business, and the fully optimized business.

The Undeveloped Business

The undeveloped business has immense potential for improvement. Maybe the owner-manager has neglected the business. Perhaps it needs refurbishment and new furniture and equipment. The capital injection will increase profits and boost the value of the going concern. Make a budget for all development costs. Introduce management controls to improve efficiency.

For every additional dollar you increase the annual profit, you increase the business value by over 2 dollars. A business can be remodeled and turned around within weeks. Later when you sell the business you will enjoy a large capital gain on the sale of your enterprise.

The Semi-developed Business

The semi-developed business provides fewer opportunities for improvement as the undeveloped business.

However, you should notice several ways to improve business performance. Usually the layout of the premises can be enhanced. Junky furniture should be replaced. Get the lighting right because it draws attention and interest. Maybe the employees need training to improve the quality of customer service.

The Fully-Optimized Business

This business is well oiled and running like clockwork. The current owner-manager has worked hard to perfect business efficiency. It is the ultimate turnkey business and you may struggle to maintain current performance. Usually these businesses sell for the highest multiple of earnings (3 - 5).

TYPE OF BUSINESS

Your optimal choice of business depends upon your knowledge and experience, and the resources you can offer the business (including funds, assets, technology and contacts).

Most businesses require a cheerful customer services oriented person to develop relationships with customers at the front end of the business; and a more logical-minded person in the back office to take care of the details. You also need a good Human Resources manager – preferably a local partner - to manage your staff.

Many successful businesspeople advise engaging in business activities you enjoy; ideally an extension of your hobby or interest. Most businesses demand a full-time commitment by the manager, particularly in the entertainment industry. Create your business to suit your personality.

Your choice of business is less important if you buy a franchise.

DO YOU NEED A WORK PERMIT?

Usually, if you want to work in your business you should obtain a work permit.

Your decision about whether to work will be influenced by the following factors:

- Your knowledge and skills
- The market value of your skills locally; unless your skills are highly specialized, you should consider delegating work to local people
- Business profitability
- The perceived value of quality time

Be aware that once you have a work permit you would normally be expected to pay taxes. Administration of work permits can be time-consuming and expensive. If you need a work permit you will probably need help from a local representative.

Consider carefully whether you really need a work permit. If you have a competent local manager or partner, maybe you only need to provide "non-executive" guidance (in which case you may not require a work permit).

ESTABLISHING AN INVESTMENT BUDGET

Establish a budget for the Total Investment in your business. The Total Investment includes the following costs:

- Legal fees relating to business transfer
- Remodeling the premises
- Rent payable in advance and security deposit
- Replacement of fixtures, fittings and equipment
- Recruitment
- Visas and work permits
- Additional working capital
- Company incorporation costs (if necessary)
- Marketing
- Business licenses (if required)

Usually rent is payable monthly in advance. In addition, the landlord often demands a security deposit to cover possible damage to the property. Lessees either claim this deposit from the subsequent owner or claim the money back from the landlord when the lease is re-assigned.

TIMING – THE BEST TIME TO START

Do not to rush into any business venture without sufficient research and professional advice. Learning the local language, culture and etiquette takes time to grasp. First of all develop strong relationships with local people and expats.

You may be ready to start your business when you have the following in place:

- A working knowledge of the local language
- An understanding of the local culture, customs and business practices
- Some local friends you can trust
- Knowledge of the legal system and how it affects foreign businesspeople
- An understanding of the market you want to target
- A researched business plan
- Sufficient liquid funds available to turn your plan into reality

You cannot plan the timing of opportunities, but you may be able to negotiate a future date of business transfer. Some owners want to sell after the close of the peak season to benefit their cash flow. Finally, the timing of your business start-up may be influenced by your own cash flow situation.

Guidelines

Do not pay money for the business until you have secured a reasonable lease with the landlord. Register the business when you start trading. Do not make the common mistake of forming a company while looking for a business to buy. Many foreigners have dormant companies because they formed limited companies and later decided not to buy a business.

HOW TO EVALUATE BUSINESSES

The Key Determinants Of Business Valuation

Business Valuation is the process of calculating the value of a going concern. Business Evaluation is a more extensive process which includes assessment of employees, the seller and his or her reason for selling, business control systems, market trends and non-financial (or qualitative) aspects of the business.

There are numerous factors influencing the business evaluation process. Examples are location, presentation, profitability, lease terms, personality of the owner and finance terms of sale. Every businessperson has different priorities. There is much more to business evaluation than just financial review.

The main factors which determine the value of a business are Total Investment, net profit (after depreciation and taxes), lease terms and an estimated value of the assets included in the sale.

Total Investment is the price paid for a business plus the additional investment necessary to achieve target performance. Total Investment includes remodelling costs, legal fees, payments to the landlord, and replacement of assets.

> Total Investment = Price paid to the seller for the business + Remodeling Costs + Legal Fees + Replacement of Assets + Rent payable in Advance + Security Deposit (if not included in the sale) + Other costs of starting up the business

Before evaluating any businesses, determine your Total Investment budget. In most developing countries businesses are transferred when the seller receives payment in cash. However sellers may be willing to negotiate credit terms of sale, typically with 50% - 75% down payment.

Net profit represents the real business earnings. The earnings include any amounts drawn from the business by the owner in the form of salary or personal (non-business) expenses. A good owner-manager will increase the net profits of the business, increasing both earnings and the value of the business simultaneously.

The earnings of the business determine the payback period of the investment. The Payback Period (in years) is the estimated period required to recover the investment by the business owner.

> Payback Period = Total Investment / Net Annual Earnings

Buyers usually demand a payback period between one and three years; Sellers usually want to sell their going concern at an equivalent payback period of between two and four years. After negotiation, the buyer and seller usually settle on a net earnings multiple of between 2.0 and 3.0. The payback period is higher for businesses that are fully developed.

The value of the assets included in the sale is most significant when the business is not trading. Usually failed businesses are sold for the value of the business assets only (without any premium for goodwill). The assets would be valued at the higher of net book value (ie after depreciation, as stated in the fixed asset register) and the market value of the equivalent second hand assets.

The most common determinants considered by business buyers are:

- Lease terms offered by the landlord
- Relationship – and level of trust and rapport – between buyer and seller
- Location of the business - is the area improving or degenerating?
- Offer price
- Business earnings and payback period
- Presentation of the business
- The value, age, and state of repair of all assets included in the sale
- Atmosphere of the business and morale of owner, customers, suppliers and employees
- Opportunities for developing the business
- Extent of training and support package offered by the seller
- The reputation of the business amongst the local businesspeople
- Business trends – Is sales turnover increasing or decreasing? Try to understand the underlying reasons for the trends
- Consider also whether the business can be easily copied or relocated

TOTAL INVESTMENT

Total Investment is the total amount of money invested in the business. The amount you invest in the business should be below your total investment budget. Total Investment is identifiable on a cash-flow statement as the maximum cash deficit.

The amount you paid to the business seller may represent say 70% of Total Investment. In addition to the purchase price, your investment budget includes the following costs:

- Legal fees relating to the business transfer
- Remodeling costs of the business premises
- Business licensing costs
- The cost of obtaining visas and work permit
- Replacement cost of fixtures, fitting and furniture
- Recruitment fees for the hiring of new staff
- Increase in working capital (including stocks and receivables)
- Any losses incurred after business transfer (if applicable)

Your Total Investment (TI) should include all expenditure necessary for the business to generate your target level of profits. The TI needs to be sufficient to fully upgrade and equip the business. Ideally, after spending the TI, your business will be self-supporting.

Exercise self-discipline with regard to your budgeted Total Investment. Decide on your maximum business investment (or TI) before you start spending money. If the business is not self-supporting after investing your TI, the business has failed or your plan has not worked out. Next, plan to minimize your losses. Avoid throwing more and more money into a bottomless investment.

If your business is successful, you will recover your total investment (with a good return) during the term of your lease. If you sell the business later, you will make a capital gain by selling above original TI.

BUSINESS VALUATION METHODS

Small businesses sold as going concerns include guest houses, restaurants, cafés, and bars. Business profitability can change dramatically – either way – after the business transfer.

A resourceful buyer can turn around a loss-making business into a profitable concern within weeks. For this reason, valuation methods for small businesses are not sophisticated. The value of small businesses is primarily determined by estimating annual profits and the value of the business assets.

A business is only worth what people pay for it. Let the buyers be the judges who vote using their wallets. If there are many similar businesses for sale in the same area, market prices fall. Unique businesses which are difficult to copy command higher prices.

US Industry surveys show that businesses sell for 75% - 80% of the seller's asking price. Many sellers list businesses with brokers at vastly inflated prices. The seller wants the broker to earn their fee by achieving higher net proceeds than would otherwise be possible. Also some "sellers" are not really serious about selling (unless a buyer pays their "fantasy" price).

If you like a business, work out what it's worth to you, and make an appropriate offer. Your broker has a professional duty to pass on all offers (supported by a deposit), even if they are relatively low. You have nothing to lose as long as you protect yourself with appropriate conditions to the offer.

Some local sellers have extremely creative valuation methods. One seller included a personal loan from his sister in his calculation of selling price. The loan had no relevance to the business. Personal financial arrangements fall outside the scope of business valuation. However if a seller is willing to offer "buyer finance", allowing payment by instalments, this can increase the selling price.

Tom West's *Complete Guide to Business Brokerage* lists the following ten key factors to consider while valuing a business: They are:

- Number of years the business has been in existence
- Number of years the seller has owned the business
- Terms offered by the seller
- Competition – How much is there in the local market?
- Risk – Is the business inherently risky?
- Growth or trend of the business sales and profits
- Location and facilities
- Desirability – How popular is the business in the current location?
- Industry – Is the industry growing or declining?
- Type of Business. Is it easily duplicated? In Asia, profitable businesses are copied in no time

Other factors to consider are:

- Sensitivity of the business to external factors such as tourism high and low seasons
- Is the rent below or above market rate? A lease offering rent below market value increases the business value
- The length of the lease - longer lease usually adds value to the business
- The skills and quality of the employees - if there is an employee you do not need, ensure the seller terminates their employment contract (and settles the severance pay) before you buy the business
- Orders received in advance increase the value of the business
- How accurate can you predict future revenues and expenses? If income and expenses are stable and predictable, the lower risk increases business value
- Does the Seller's personality influence the success of the business? Do customers come to the business to see the seller or because they like the product itself? Will you retain the existing customer base?
- How old is the equipment, and when will it need replacing?
- Is the Seller willing to offer sufficient training and support during the initial period after business transfer?

Multiple of Adjusted Net Profits

Many business brokers value businesses using a multiple of three times adjusted annual net profits. Most businesses actually sell for about 2 times the seller's adjusted net profits. This means that the business should pay for itself within two years.

Adjusted Net Profits is the earnings, after paying all operational overheads, including depreciation of fixed assets. Any non-business costs must be added back to the seller's profit. For example, if the owner's spouse was paid a monthly salary without actually working for the business, this item should be added back to the net profit figure.

Depreciation is a method of accounting for the cost of wear and tear of the fixed assets (such as machinery, vehicles, equipment, computers, fixture and fittings). This allowance for "wear and tear" of fixed assets is usually applied on a "straight line" basis over the estimated life of the assets.

If a computer is purchased for US$1,000 and it has an estimated product life of 3 years, the annual depreciation charge is US$333. Deduct US$333 from the seller's net profit to allow for replacement of the computer.

Any drawings from the business - or salary paid to the owner who is not working for the business - should be added back to the net profits. Only legitimate business expenses should be deducted from earnings to arrive at adjusted net profits.

Mini-marts

Mini-marts are sometimes valued at a multiple of between 1.0 and 1.25 times adjusted net profits plus the stock at valuation (SAV) on the date of business transfer. SAV is always the actual amount paid for the stock, though sometimes it is marked down from selling price, by applying the gross profit margin. If you purchase a mini-mart, supervise the inventory count immediately before completion of business transfer.

Multiples of Gross Sales

Some business consultants use a specific multiple of gross sales to value each type of business. Examples follow:

Travel agencies:	0.05 to 0.1 X Annual Gross Sales
Advertising agencies:	0.75 X Annual Gross Sales
Retail businesses:	[0.75 to 1.5 X Annual Net Profit] + Inventory + Equipment

Estimate the net book value of the tangible business assets included in the sale. Write off the value of any old assets which require replacement. The assets may include air conditioners and the security deposit held with the landlord (if the seller has agreed to include this in the sale price).

ADJUSTMENT OF NET ANNUAL PROFITS

The following example demonstrates how the Net Annual Profits figure is adjusted to calculate the real earnings of the business:

INCOME	$
Sales	71,500
Other Income	16
TOTAL INCOME	71,516
COST OF GOODS SOLD	40,241
GROSS PROFIT (43.7%)	31,275
EXPENSES	
Rent	3,086
Salaries	18,648
Outside labour	1,600
Social Insurance	214
Electricity	129
Water	36
Telephone	1,202
Travel	1,933
Legal fees	162
Accounting fees	371
Interest	10
Bad debts	76
Miscellaneous	588
TOTAL EXPENSES	28,055
NET PROFIT BEFORE TAX	3,220

NET PROFIT BEFORE TAX	3,220
Adjustments to Profit:	
Add back Owner's salary	20,571
Add back legal fee which relate to owner's personal expense	162
Subtract: interest received	-16
Subtract: Depreciation of Fixed assets	-3,346
ADJUSTED NET PROFITS	20,591
BUSINESS VALUATION	
1. Multiple of 2.0	41,182
(Recover investment in 2 years)	
2. Multiple of 3.0	61,773
(Recover investment in 3 years)	

If you need to recover your investment over two years, you may pay as much as US$41,182 for the business. This price includes all the business assets necessary to operate the business. If the seller excludes specific assets from the sale you should deduct the cost of replacing these assets.

Discounted Cash Flow

Discounted Net Present Value (NPV), or discounted cash flow, is a more sophisticated method of business valuation suited to larger business organisations. The annual cash flows (both inflows and outflows) are discounted using the investors discount factor or "cost of money". The discount factor is usually equal to the cost of borrowing (if applicable) or the return on investment required by the investor.

Example: US$30,000 receivable in twelve months would have a net present value (NPV) of US$27,272 if the business owner's cost of money is 10%. The NPV is the cash received divided by $(1 + X)$, where X is the discount factor. This valuation method, however, is usually too sophisticated for small businesses where cash flows cannot be forecast with sufficient accuracy.

Return on Investment

Aim to maximize your return on your investment and remunerate yourself for any services rendered for your business.

Aim to recover your total investment together with a return (or profit) during the period of your lease. Although you may sell your business at a profit, it's prudent to recover your investment before you sell the business.

If you work for the business, give yourself a salary at market rate and claim any business-related expenses. For financial purposes, treat yourself as separate from your business. This means that your investment in the business is like a personal loan to the business. Similarly, your salary from the business is comparable to remuneration from any third party employer.

Your target return on investment depends upon the risk of your business. A low risk business, like rental property, should return over 10% per annum. A business with average risk, like a restaurant, may require a return of 20-30% per annum. A highly risky business may require a return of over 100% per annum. Don't forget you need a higher return than 4%+ - which your bank may offer you for investing your cash in a savings account.

INVESTMENT	YIELD RANGE
Cash in Bank Current Account	0%
Cash in Bank Savings Account	1% - 5%
Property Investment	3%-14%
Mutual Funds	8%-30+%
Business valued at 3 x Earnings	33%
Business with 2 year Payback Period	50%
Business with 12 month Payback Period	100%

CASE STUDY: Bill invests US$58,000 in a guest house business. He does not work for the guest house business, so he does not claim a "salary". He requires a return on investment of 20% over his three year lease. This means that Bill needs to recover his capital at a rate of US$19,333 per annum (US$58,000/3) plus an average return of US$5,800 per annum (because the average capital outstanding over the term of the lease is US$29,000). Bill needs total profits of US$75,400 over the three year period, or an average of US$25,133 per annum. Therefore, if the guest house generates less than US$25,133 profit per year, Bill would reject the investment. Any proceeds from the subsequent sale of the guest house would increase the return on investment accordingly.

Payback Period

The Payback Period is the time taken (in years) to recover your investment in the business from net adjusted profits. A short payback period of between six months and 2.5 years attracts prospective buyers; whereas a longer payback period of over 3 years is more attractive to sellers.

> Payback Period (in years) = Investment / Adjusted Net Annual Profits

The Payback Period is equal to the price actually paid for the business (after discount) divided by the adjusted net profits. The business broker and seller calculate the payback period using the price offered for the business; but the buyer's real payback period is increased by any additional costs of investment (such as interior decoration and replacement of furniture and equipment).

LEASE TERMS

Evaluating the Lease

The lease for your business premises is a fundamental part of the business. A good lease provides security of tenure for a reasonable period with inexpensive rent.

Engage your local representative or lawyer in all negotiations with the landlord.

Rent Level

Usually the landlord increases the rent whenever there is a change of lessee. You can make an offer for a business conditional on a maximum rent level. If the current owner leases the premises for US$400 per month, you may make an offer subject to a maximum monthly rent of US$450 for the following three years, with a reasonable renewal option.

Research the market rents in the local area. Real estate agents in the neighborhood should provide the information you need. Don't forget that long leases with low rent potentially increase the value of the business (and vice versa).

Lease Term

Leases in prime locations may be (short) one year renewable contacts requiring payment of the years rent in advance. You may be able to negotiate a long commercial lease of ten years or more. Remember that a longer lease adds value to your business.

Check whether it is beneficial to register the lease at the local land registry.

Registering the Lease in Your Company's Name

It can be advantageous contracting with your landlord using a limited company. It may be easier to transfer your business to a third party in the future by selling your company shares to the buyer. This way, the corporate lessee does not change. The buyer takes over the existing lease, so there should be no surprise hike in rent. Instruct your lawyer to check the lease for clauses relating to business transfer. The contract may require the landlord's approval of the new company director (and shareholder).

Security Deposit

The landlord may require a security deposit against damage of the property and his or her furniture and equipment. The deposit is usually between one and six months rent. Many landlords find it difficult to return deposits, but don't mind them being used to pay the final period of rent. The seller may include the security deposit in the selling price of the business, so it is effectively transferred to the new tenant. This matter should be covered in the negotiations with the seller.

Remodeling the Premises

If you intend to make any structural changes to the property, you must get the landlord's written permission beforehand. Try to obtain the landlord's permission in the lease agreement. If the premises are to be developed, any changes are likely to benefit the landlord. The landlord must understand that you want to increase the value of the property.

Rent Review

Your offer to purchase the business may be conditional upon the landlord not increasing the rent by more than a specified amount during a defined period.

Assignment of the Lease

Check all clauses in the lease which may potentially prevent you from assigning the lease to a prospective buyer in the future. Usually landlords prepare new leases with higher rent when a business is transferred. This is a common cause of buyers withdrawing their offer to purchase a business. Consider how you might assign your lease in the future, so you can sell the business for a reasonable price.

LOCATION

Most successful retailers advise never to compromise on location. Choose a busy location which is favored by your target customers.

There are many factors which influence whether a customer visits a shop. The main determinants are:

- Premises situated on the corner of road junctions are favorable because they benefit from additional side access
- Shops which are opened up to the street (with less wall area) are more inviting to prospective customers
- Lighter units are more attractive to clientele than poorly light shops, so optimize window area and lighting
- Attract the interest of your target customers by displaying eye-catching bold signage outside your premises
- Consider wide shop units because they offer additional access to passing trade
- Optimize every square meter of space to generate maximum profit; get redundant areas working for you. Ensure your lease allows you to make the necessary modifications to the premises

It's easy to assess location; one method is to employ someone to count the potential customers passing your proposed location; and counting customers visiting your nearest competitor. Note the type of customers frequenting the area, the proportion of foreign tourists, their age and estimated disposable incomes. Some audacious potential buyers ask the competitors' manager to show them their sales day book; and usually they get what thy want.

THE SELLER

It is important that you trust the seller. Establishing a good rapport with the seller is a great advantage because you will receive more support (or training) during the early stages of trading.

Some sellers misrepresent their financial accounts, overstating gross sales and understating business expenses. It's the buyer's responsibility to validate all representations made by the seller. Obtain written confirmation that the seller will assume his or her business liabilities at the date of transfer. For example, the electricity bill for the business should be apportioned between buyer and seller.

If any of the seller's financial representations do not make sense, ask questions and demand satisfactory answers. You may have legitimate grounds for negotiating a lower price, possibly subject to credit terms.

To help avoid the possibility of the business vendor setting up a similar business opposite your new business and poaching your employees and customers, ask him or her to sign a non-competition clause in the offer document.

Usually sellers agree not to compete in a similar business within a 2km radius of your business for at least 2 years.

Understand the real reason for the sale before you buy the business. Get third party confirmation and evidence to support the seller's story. You don't want to start your new business feeling you have been duped by the seller.

MORALE

The morale in the business is important. This includes the mood of the owner, the customers, suppliers and employees. Sometimes the owner has given up on the exhausted business and the employees adopt the same negative attitude. Clearly there is a lot of work to be done to turn around such a business.

Try to discover the inherent problems. Are you able to correct these issues? Or is there a fundamental problem outside your control, like a troublesome landlord or severe competition taking away customers?

ASSET SALE

Some "businesses" for sale have actually ceased trading. After a business closes down, the selling price should be usually based on the value of the business assets transferable.

Consider the prospective project as a start-up situation. It may take you over twelve months before the business breaks even. Sometimes businesspeople are willing to pay a large premium for an empty shop in a good location.

Usually asset sales occur in poor locations rather than prime business spots.

Obtain a list of the business assets, including stock, and work out what they are worth to you. Items which need replacing are worth nothing. It is helpful to have the following information for fixed assets: description of asset, date of acquisition, purchase price, estimated life (in years) and the net book value of the asset (after accumulated depreciation).

CASE STUDY: A bar, which closed down recently, is available for sale. It is in a good tourist location and the premises are leased at low rent. The premium for the lease is valued at US$3,000. Most of the furniture is dilapidated and will need replacing. The only items of value are three air conditioners which are two years old and a music system. A buyer offers US$1,500 - or half the current replacement cost – for the three air conditioners. The business seller agreed to keep the music system for himself. The buyer negotiated a total price of US$5,500 to take over the lease, the security deposit (US$1,000) and the air conditioners (US$1,500).

Sometimes sellers present their business as a going concern, when they are not trading any longer. Check the business at different times of the day and week. Don't limit your business visits to times arranged by the seller. Perhaps the seller arranged a party with his friends and family to coincide with your visit?

Lease Premium

The lease premium represents a surcharge for goodwill associated with the location of the premises and the opportunity to access passing trade. If the monthly rent payable is below the market rate, the premium is higher.

NOTE: You can often avoid paying any lease premium by contracting directly with the landlord.

THE REASON FOR SALE

The most important question to ask the business seller is *"Why do you want to sell?"* Nothing else matters until you understand why the seller wants to part with the business. Ask the vital question after you have established a rapport with the seller.

The 5 main reasons for the sale of a business are:

- Burnout, health, partnership problems or desire for change in lifestyle (common in the restaurant trade)
- Retirement; but if it's a good business why is the seller not keeping it in the family?
- Poor business or problems with the landlord
- The seller is not really serious about selling unless they receive their fantasy price
- The seller wants to realize the capital gain, take a holiday, and then start all over again (in this case, be careful not to lose your customers and employees)

Below I explain in detail the responses to the golden question: *"Why do you want to sell your business?"* Some answers are absurd but I will stick to the usual replies.

Partnership Problems

Sometimes the joint investors disagree on key management issues. However, this usually happens when the business is underperforming. If the business is doing well, what is there to argue about?

Health Problems

Some sellers are forced to sell due to severe health problems. The shock of a heart attack may be the catalyst causing a major shift in lifestyle.

One businessman, who ran several successful service businesses, experienced major health problem requiring surgery. Immediately he placed all of his businesses on the market for sale. His businesses were genuinely profitable.

This reason for sale is usually quite easy to validate. Many of the neighboring businesspeople probably knew about the operation and some may have visited him in the hospital.

Not enough Time

Two common answers are *"Not enough time"* and *"Need to spend time on other businesses."* Both answers are unconvincing. If a businessperson is leaving the business alone because they are preoccupied with other businesses, it's probably an under-performing business. If the seller does not have enough time, find out what they do allow time for. Usually these sellers have given up on the business and have started another one.

"I need more Quality Time"

Some semi-retired people buy a business to occupy their time and alleviate boredom. Usually they discover to their peril that the business is much more demanding than they ever expected. The business may have potential, but they don't have the energy to exploit the opportunity. The seller's reason for sale may be genuine, but get confirmation.

Relocation

Many sellers say they want to relocate to another city, or even another continent. A death in the family or severe sickness of a relative may give reason for rapid departure. If the reason given is genuine, they would probably want to sell quickly at a low price. Most sellers wanting out of the business and the city have some serious problems which they may not be willing to discuss.

DUE DILIGENCE

Due Diligence is the process of substantiating the seller's representations, including the financial statements. Due diligence is the buyer's responsibility. Business brokers do not have any responsibility for checking the information they pass on from seller to buyer unless they have reason to believe it to be misleading or false.

Many small businesses in developing countries do not keep any business records or accounts. Businesses may simply negotiate a tax settlement with a tax officer once a year. Some businesses maintain three sets of accounting records, one set for the authorities (to minimize tax), another record for potential investors, and a record of the actual transactions (for themselves).

One practical way of checking gross sales is to employ a person to count the number of customers visiting the business.

> Daily Sales = Number of Customers x Estimated Average Sales Value

Estimate the average gross sales value per customer transaction. The business seller may provide this information, but watch what the customers order and estimate the average transaction value.

Take account of the time of year. If the business is tourism-oriented, consider estimating annual gross sales in the following way:

> Annual Sales = [4 x Monthly Sales in LS] + [8 x Monthly Sales in HS]

LS = Low Season
HS = High Season

The sales in the high season may be three times that of sales in low season. Estimate this multiple with the help of businesspeople in the neighborhood. The seller may provide an accurate multiple.

Continue due diligence testing until you are reasonably sure of the actual business performance. However, if the business is underperforming and you intend to develop the business, future results may improve significantly.

Do not instruct any advisors who are directly connected with either business broker or seller, to avoid any possible conflict of interests. For larger businesses, hire an independent consultant, accountant and lawyer to audit the business financials.

Do not complete the business transfer until you have sufficient evidence to support the seller's financial representations. If you have evidence that the seller has misrepresented the performance of the business, renegotiate or withdraw your offer (and reclaim any deposit paid). After transfer of the business it's too late to claim recourse; the seller may be sipping champagne in Hawaii by then.

THE BUSINESS EVALUATION CHECKLIST

Before you hand over your life savings to the seller, make sure you have evaluated the business thoroughly. Try this checklist:

Business Location

Is the business location suitable for your purposes? Don't forget that being only 30 meters away from a "good location" may be too far without a sound marketing strategy.

The Landlord

Are the lease terms reasonable? Is the remaining term of the lease long enough to recover your investment and make a reasonable return on your investment? Is there evidence that the landlord will maintain the property according to the lease terms? Have you checked the rent level against market rent for similar properties in the area?

The Seller

Do you have a good rapport with, and trust, the seller? Why is the business owner selling? Is the customer base loyal to the seller, the business or the product?

Accounts

Has your due diligence and research supported the seller's representations and financial statements? If there are no proper accounts available, have you prepared your own budgetary forecasts?

Legal Structure of Acquisition

Are you buying the assets of the business, or are you buying shares in the seller's company (which owns the business assets)? If you need a work permit there are advantages of taking over the seller's limited company. This avenue will save you Government stamp duty, time and lawyer's fees; also because the lessee does not change, dealings with the landlord may be more straightforward. It may save you a rent increase and transfer fees too.

Environment

Do you like the environment of the business? If you will be working full-time, or even part-time, you must like being there.

CASE STUDY (ASSET SALE)

The following case study is typical of the listings published on the internet:

A partnership dispute forces the sale of this six month old beauty Salon. The business is offered for sale at asset value. The shop measures 40 square metres and is located in a shopping mall near the city centre. The partners spent US$22,500 on fixed assets and US$8,500 on inventory. The salon has been well promoted and has its own website. There is a growing loyal customer base. The gross sales forecast for the first year is US$43,000. Monthly rent is $685 and monthly salaries total US$675 for three full time employees. There is ample parking space for customers. The salon offers a full range of beauty services including massage and reflexology. Asking Price: US$28,500

Projected Profits for the first 12 Months (US$)

Sales		43,000
Rent	8,220	
Payroll	8,100	
Depreciation	7,500	
($22,500 of assets over three years)		
Cost of consumables	8,500	
Services	1,700	
Accounts & legal	1,450	
Total Costs		35,470
Estimated Net Profit		7,530

The net profit is apportioned between two partners. Each partner is expecting to receive US$3,765 each year.

If the partners aim to recover their capital of US$31,000 over a three year period with a return of 20%, they need net profits of US$13,433 each year (compared to US$7,530).

If the business generates net annual profits of US$7,530, the business would take over four years to pay back their investment without any return. Clearly the partners would argue less if they had invested their money elsewhere.

Conclusion

The above business failed. The investors want to cut their losses and get out as quickly as possible. They are open to any offers.

If you or your spouse is knowledgeable of this trade, the location is good and the lease terms are reasonable, consider making a low offer for the business assets. Make a list of the assets you want, estimate their purchase prices and offer a proportion of the total depending on the condition of the assets. The sellers may eventually give the assets away - or even pay someone to remove them.

PROPERTY PRICES

If you want to "buy" land or buildings you must consider property values separate from the value of the business. If the buildings are old, and you need to demolish them, research the market value of the land and the cost of demolition or removal of waste.

Land prices vary enormously from province to province, from city center to rural areas and even within confined areas.

CAUTION: In many countries it is unlawful for foreigners to buy land. However there are usually legal "loopholes" which enable you enjoy the rights associated with owning the property. Ask a reputable legal advisor for guidance about owning property.

THE STAGES OF BUYING A BUSINESS

The key stages of buying a business are:

- Defining your objectives
- Research
- Sourcing businesses
- Business evaluation
- Offer to purchase
- Negotiation
- Due diligence
- Completion

Defining your Objectives

Be clear about what you want to give – and take from – the business. Below is a list of questions to ask:

- What is your total investment budget for the business?
- What is your role in the business?
- What is your required payback period and return?
- Which types of business will you consider?
- Which locations will you consider?

Research

During the research stage you should become familiar with local culture and etiquette. Get a working knowledge of the language. Meet the businesspeople and find out how business in done locally. Identify suitable businesses for sale on the internet.

SOURCING BUSINESSES

If you are good at networking and independent research, sourcing businesses for sale is straightforward. Ask as many businesspeople and expats as possible about businesses available for sale. Many expats and locals have friends who want to sell a business. The introducer may receive a small referral commission from the seller.

Don't restrict your search to businesses which are actively marketed for sale. Some businesses for sale remain on the market for years because they are ridiculously overpriced.

A good starting point is the online listings of local business brokers. Note down the reference of any listings which interest you and view them. Also check private classified advertisements in local newspapers and websites.

Businesses for sale sometimes display a "For Sale" sign outside their shop, but these owners are usually desperate to sell. Also check local public notice boards. If you see any potential in one of these businesses for sale, work out what it is worth to you, discount the number, and make an offer. The sight of crisp bank notes usually facilitates a quick decision by the seller.

Direct canvassing of specific businesses in targeted locations can be very effective. If you know what you want, there are few businesses to target. A buyer might approach 15 guest houses in the same area on the same day. Exchange name cards with each owner and follow up a few days later.

LOOKING FOR SUITABLE PREMISES

Allow at least six months to find suitable premises. There is intense competition for prime business locations. Tenants in the best locations are approached by prospective tenants almost daily.

There are two ways to find suitable premises: using a broker or by direct contact with landlords. Business brokers sell businesses rather than acting as agents for a commercial property rentals agency. Some real estate agencies list commercial rentals.

First decide what type of premises you want, and its size and location. Talk to many business people in the target neighborhood. Conduct your search with a local representative. Some people hire opportunistic tuk-tuk (taxi) drivers to drive them to suitable commercial rental properties. Look out for "For Rent" signs. Check the classifieds in local newspapers.

Check the market rents in the surrounding area. Make sure your landlord gives you written permission to modify the property as necessary. Does the landlord meet his or her responsibilities by repairing the property; or has water been leaking through the ceiling for years? Are future

95

rent increases limited in the lease agreement (eg a 10% increase after 3 years)?

Usually businesses for sale require the assignment of an existing lease or the preparation of a new lease. Negotiate a new lease with the landlord (with the support of your representative). Leases registered in a company name simply involve a change of shareholder.

Leasehold Improvements

Any leasehold improvements, fixtures and fittings usually revert to the ownership of the landlord when the lease expires. Therefore, write off the cost of leasehold improvements over the period of the lease. Any improvements to the property potentially add value to your business by increasing sales and the selling price.

Serviced Offices

Serviced offices are suitable for many professional service businesses such as real estate brokers, where location is less important. Serviced office providers do not demand a premium payable to the landlord, sometimes called "key money". Usually serviced offices provide photocopying and fax facilities as well as secretarial services. Although rent may be higher, serviced offices minimise the tenant's investment during the initial stages of start-up.

Shopping Malls

Many shopping malls operate a voucher system for cash receipts. The customer buys vouchers from a kiosk which are exchanged for meals at any of the surrounding food counters. Any unused vouchers are refundable at the kiosk.

The shopping malls normally charge 25% – 35% of the licensee's gross receipts. The mall pays the business licensee the net receipts some two months afterwards. Although the licensees can generate good sales, it is necessary to finance two months Cost of Sales.

HOW TO DEAL WITH SELLERS

The main objective of the first meeting with the seller is to establish rapport with the seller. Without rapport, the seller will not offer the information and support you need. Leave the detailed financial questions for later.

Observe everything around you while establishing rapport with the seller. Use all your senses: sight, hearing, smell, intuition, and taste (if the seller is a restaurateur)! What is the mood of the staff and customers?

Ask the seller "open" questions and let him or her do most of the talking. Find out why the business is for sale and what are the seller's plans?

Selling a business can be nerve-wracking, especially when providing private information to people who may not be genuine. Be sensitive to the seller's predicament and demonstrate interest in the business. If you enjoy friendly conversation over a drink with the seller, you have achieved the objective of the initial meeting.

THE OFFER TO PURCHASE

The Offer Price

How much is the business worth to you? Try the following formula to estimate an appropriate offer price:

> Offer Price = [Payback Period (years) x Adjusted Net Profits (real earnings)] – [Additional Costs]

The payback period (in years) is the maximum period required to recover the total investment.

Additional costs include property refurbishment, replacement of furniture and equipment, and advances to the landlord.

EXAMPLE: John wants to recover his investment within a two year period. The real earnings of the guesthouse are US$40,000 per annum. He estimates additional costs, including replacement of furniture, to be US$10,000. Using the above formula, his offer price would be US$70,000.

Direct Offers

If you make a direct offer to a business owner (without an agent), do not support your offer with a deposit unless you are prepared to lose the money. If the seller is unscrupulous he or she may accept a higher offer the next day, and it may be difficult to recover the deposit.

You need to convince the seller that you are a serious buyer and have the funds. After establishing the terms of the new lease, arrange a meeting between your local representative, seller and landlord. Exchange your certified bank check for a signed lease and specified business assets.

Offers via Brokers

The Offer to Purchase marks the beginning of negotiations. The business broker prepares the offer document on behalf of the buyer. The offer is accompanied by the buyer's deposit (of between 10% and 20% of price offered). Your broker will tell you that an offer without a deposit is not a real offer.

The offer provides the names and addresses of buyer and seller, the date of offer and proposed date of completion. The document also states the price offered for the business, the deposit paid and balance payable. Assets included in the sale are specified (such as furniture, fittings, equipment, trademarks, goodwill and inventory). All business liabilities remain the responsibility of the seller unless agreed otherwise.

Most Offers to Purchase a business stipulate the following specific conditions:

- Landlord's permission to modify the property as required
- The maximum acceptable rent on the new lease
- The minimum lease term
- The landlord's security deposit is included in the selling price
- No competition by seller in a similar trade within a radius of 2 kilometers of premises for two years
- Training and support for two weeks after transfer of business

- Seller is responsible for the payment of all business liabilities on the date of completion
- Seller agrees to finance the transaction, for example, by accepting 60% down payment with the balance payable in two equal instalments, 3 months and 6 months after completion
- Seller agrees to allow buyer access to all accounting and financial records between offer and completion dates
- Seller agrees to terminate the employment of (name of employee) before completion; buyer will reimburse legal cost of severance
- Seller agrees to include a minimum value of inventory in the sale

Your broker takes your signed offer to the seller. There are three possible outcomes: acceptance, outright rejection or counter-offer. There are many variables to negotiate with other than price including exclusion of security deposit or specified assets, and buyer finance (or credit terms).

Once the offer has been agreed and signed by both parties, it is the seller's responsibility to meet the conditions of offer. If the seller does not comply with your offer terms, the broker should return your deposit in full. **You must complete your due diligence and validation of the seller's representations before completion of the sale**. If the buyer can show evidence of misrepresentation by the seller, the offer is annulled.

A common obstacle in business transfer is the landlord increasing the rent to a level unacceptable to the buyer. Sometimes the landlord is not prepared to offer long enough lease terms to suit the buyer.

Obtain a detailed list of all assets included in the sale, signed and dated by the seller. Go through this list, item by item, and estimate the value of each asset before completion.

ARE YOU READY TO MAKE AN OFFER? (A CHECKLIST)

The Offer to Purchase

- Have you considered making an offer conditional on the seller offering terms of finance?
- Have you decided upon all the other conditions of your offer?

The Seller

- Do you trust the business vendor?
- Do you believe their reason for selling?
- Does the seller have daily accounting records to show you?

Premises

- Is the location suitable for your purpose?
- Are the proposed lease terms acceptable?
- Is the rent reasonable compared to average market value?
- Is the guaranteed lease term long enough to recover your investment?
- Have you obtained estimates of refurbishment?
- Does the landlord allow structural modifications to the premises?
- Are there any clauses in the lease relating to the future

assignment of the lease to a new tenant?
- Will your local limited company be the lessee?
- Does the selling price include the security deposit held by the landlord?

Investment

- Is the estimated total investment (including remodelling costs and replacement of business assets) within your budget?
- Will you have the necessary liquid funds available on the date of completion?

Business Assets

- Which assets do you need, and which are included in the sale price?
- Which assets on the premises are owned by the landlord, the seller (personally) or another third party?
- Have you obtained estimates of all furniture, fittings and equipment which need replacing?

Employees

- Are there any employees working for the seller who are not suitable for your business?

COMPLETION

Completion proceeds after the conditions of the Offer to Purchase have been fulfilled and the seller's representations have been validated by the buyer. The date of completion is the cut-off point for due diligence.

The key stages of completion (in order) are:

- Signing of a new lease by buyer and landlord; buyer pays rent in advance and security deposit to the landlord
- Agreement of the terms of business transfer
- Buyer pays agreed purchase price to seller by bank check or in cash and receives a written receipt

The business transfer is complete when:

- The new lease has been agreed and signed by buyer and landlord
- The business transfer agreements (including Asset Transfer Agreement) have been signed by buyer and seller
- The seller has complied with all conditions of the offer
- The seller has agreed to settle all liabilities of the business as at the date of completion
- The buyer is satisfied that all fixed assets and inventory included in the sale are on the premises
- The buyer pays the seller for the business
- If you use the broker's in-house lawyer, they will probably insist you sign legal disclaimers availing them of any legal responsibility

Attend the completion meeting with a totally reliable local representative or lawyer. Your colleague must check the property registration documents against the landlord's ID card and the lease contract. Sometimes "the landlord" is actually a sub-lessee. If he or she says they "forgot to bring the property registration documents to the meeting," do not proceed.

Obtain signed copies of the ID cards of both landlord and seller. Bring your passport to the meeting together with copies for the landlord and the seller

The buyer is advised to pay the seller by banker's check. Sometimes sellers ask for payment in cash. If necessary arrange for the payment of cash on your bank's premises. The seller will probably discourage completion on Sunday or public holidays when the banks are closed because they want their money banked as soon as possible.

RECRUITING STAFF

Employ committed staff with good character and personality. Check work references of prospective employees. Many expats make the mistake of not checking references properly. It is usually much more difficult firing ineffective employees than hiring them.

PREVENTING THEFT

Retail businesses are most vulnerable to theft by customers and employees. The extent of theft depends upon the management of the business.

The 3 key ways of preventing theft and fraud are:

- Implementation of internal control procedures
- Segregation of duties between different employees
- Office policy agreed and signed by each employee

Internal Controls

Internal controls are procedures adopted to prevent errors, inefficiencies or losses.

Examples of internal controls are:

- Monthly bank reconciliations to identify any differences between transactions recorded in the cashbook and the bank statement
- Reimbursement of expenses following sight of original purchase receipt and purchase requisition (previously budgeted and signed by a manager)
- Directors or owners sign all company checks once a week and the manager is responsible for the petty cash
- Publicize the termination of employment of senior employees
- Encourage customers to pay by credit card or check instead of cash
- Written quotations signed by the manager before submitting them to customers
- Disallow staff to benefit from obsolete or damaged goods
- Regular stock counts to compare gross profit margins each month
- Reconciliation between purchase ledger and supplier statements
- Ensure every employee takes a holiday each year
- Regular banking of cash and use of a secure safe
- Closed circuit TV deters theft in retails outlets
- Sequential numbering in date order of all invoices and order forms
- Keep the company checkbook and block stamp in a locked drawer
- Never write a check without supporting original invoices and evidence of delivery; stamp "PAID" on the invoice and note the check number on it.

105

Segregation of Duties

Reduce the opportunity for fraud by segregating duties among staff in the following ways:

- Keep responsibility for production (or service fulfillment) separate from accounting and sales
- Keep responsibility for purchasing separate from sales
- Ideally there would be different departments for cash receipts, cash payments, purchasing, sales and service fulfillment; but this is not possible in most small businesses.
- Ideally the business owner is responsible for ordering all goods from established suppliers.
- Fast food restaurants can prevent theft by having a cashier taking payments in advance; then meals are dispensed upon presentation of printed receipts. No receipt, no meal.

Office Policy

The office policy must be discussed at a staff meeting, properly explained and agreed (in writing) by all members of the staff. Ideally your local partner will deal with these sensitive matters. Every employee needs to understand the benefits of the office policy; do not collect signatures until everyone genuinely agrees with it.

In many parts of Asia the biggest issue to contend with concerns "gifts", tips and kickbacks given to members of the staff. Typical clauses in the office policy dealing with this matter are:

Any freelance work conducted by employees outside of the company must be reported to the manager

There should never be a conflict of interest between employment and freelance activity outside the company

All tips, kickbacks and gifts must be reported to, and approved by, the manager; failure to do so results in immediate dismissal

All office documents remain in the office at all times

Some companies pool all tips and gifts given to staff and they are shared equally.

CHAPTER 4: BUYING A FRANCHISE

INTRODUCTION

Many successfully branded businesses are available worldwide as franchises. Although investment in a franchise is higher than an independent business, the risk (of failure) is much lower. The franchisor usually charges the franchisee royalties on gross sales in return for management support and a share of marketing expenditure.

There are basically two types of franchise. Either the franchisee contracts directly with the original franchise owner or with a master franchisor. A master franchisor is able to promote sub-franchise agreements in their designated territory. For example a master franchise may cover Southeast Asia, so the master franchisor is allowed to sell franchises in any of these countries. Generally franchisees experience less risk when contracting directly with the original franchisor.

Please refer to the *Glossary of Terms* for definitions used in this chapter.

ARE YOU A SUITABLE FRANCHISEE?

Be realistic about your suitability as a franchisee. To be a successful franchisee you need to be a committed team player with sufficient funding for the business. Prior industry experience is less important than attitude and commitment. Some franchisors actually prefer their franchisees to have no directly relevant experience in the business because re-training "mature people" can be an arduous challenge.

Individuality

Do you always insist upon doing things your own way or are you comfortable following someone else's procedures? Successful franchisees are usually more team-oriented than individual. Franchisees are obligated to conform to the franchisor's established systems and procedures (as stated in their operations manual). Adherence to the systems ensures uniformity throughout the franchise network. If you prefer to devise your own systems and product lines you may not be an appropriate franchisee; if so, maybe you should consider starting your own business or buying an independent going concern.

Total Investment

Sufficient funding is essential for a franchised outlet. The franchisor will provide the business know-how, systems, training and use of the trademark but the franchisee funds the operation of the outlet. The Total Investment includes not only the franchise license fee, but also any leasehold improvements, lease security deposit, capital expenditure and working capital requirements. For example, the Total Investment of a 7-Eleven franchise may be US$ 100,000, half of which is accounted for by the franchise license fee. The franchisor usually discourages the franchisee from getting a loan to finance the investment because the loan interest increases the possibility of failure.

Objectives

What are your objectives in becoming a franchisee? If it is simply to get a good return on your investment, then a franchise may not be the right investment tool for you. A franchise is an active investment that requires the franchisee's participation in management. There are other less demanding investment vehicles than a franchise. Get involved in a franchise if you want to get a good return in the process of running an ongoing business.

FRANCHISE EVALUATION CHECKLIST

Concept

When looking into a company for possible franchising, first of all, look into the product or service. Before you look into the details of their franchise program, understand the total concept first. What is unique about their concept? How is it different from the rest? Before you become a franchisee, you should first become a customer. Do you like the product? Are they marketing an innovative product or service? Even if there are similar products in the market, what makes this company different? What makes them special? Is it the product quality? The price or the service quality? Only after you have understood the concept and have become a satisfied customer should you begin to examine their franchise offering. If you are not sold on the concept, you will be hard-pressed to sell it to your future customers.

Total Investment

Find out what the Initial Investment amount quoted by the Franchisor covers. It typically includes franchise fee, initial inventory, equipment, and renovation. Franchisees often need additional capital. Other initial investment costs include training expenses, rent deposits, business permits

& licenses, grand opening expenses, and working capital. With these additional investment costs, will the investment payback be significantly longer than the figure quoted by the franchisor in his franchise literature?

The cost of a franchise varies enormously from business to business. Upfront franchise fees range from US$1,000 to over US$500,000. What the franchise fee actually includes is another matter which varies between franchisors.

Training and Support

What type of support will the franchisor give? The franchisor can assist you in all stages of operating the business - site selection, lease negotiation, training, construction, procurement, grand opening planning, personnel recruitment, etc. After your outlet has opened, how often will the franchisor visit you for support? How often do you need to attend training programs after opening?

Franchise Agreement

The Franchise Agreement is the contract between the franchisor and the franchisee. It enumerates the rights and obligations of both parties in the relationship. It covers the beginning, the length of the term, the renewal provisions and the end of the contract.

Important provisions that should be examined in detail are the territory granted, fees & payment schedule, and conditions resulting in breach or eventual termination of the agreement. In most reasonable franchise relationships, the franchise agreement, once signed, is put away and the parties manage the relationship through mutually beneficial business practices.

Other Considerations

Below is a checklist of questions for researching each franchise business:

- How long has the franchisor been in this type of business, and when did they start franchising?
- How many franchises do they operate and where?
- How many of their outlets are owned by the original franchisor?
- Is it possible to buy an existing store instead of starting a new business?
- Can the franchise guarantee uniform quality throughout its franchise network?
- Does the franchise have an *Operational Procedures Manual* to facilitate quality control and consistency throughout the franchise network?
- What is the franchisor's fee for the franchise license, and what does the fee include?
- Is the franchise brand name registered with the Department of Trade and Industry?
- Would it be possible to meet the existing franchisees to discuss their business?
- Is the franchise registered with The International Franchise Association (IFA)?
- Does the franchise agreement allow the transfer of the franchise license, and if so, what is the transfer fee? Are there any other penalties for termination of the franchise license?
- Is the franchise ISO (International Standards Organisation) registered?

- What control procedures does the franchise have?
- What promotional support is offered by the franchisor, on and after opening the new store?
- Does the franchisor offer exclusive territorial rights?
- Which territories are available and which ones have been assigned?
- Is it permissible to spend a few days observing the operations of an existing franchise?
- What are the estimated costs of remodeling the premises, inventory and other working capital requirements?
- How does the purchasing and stock control system operate?
- Is the franchisee bound to procure all inventories from the franchisor?
- What royalties are payable to the franchisor, and when are they payable?
- What joint national marketing is organized by the franchisor and how is it charged to the franchisees?
- What are the operating sales and profits of the stores and would it be possible to obtain financial statements?
- Have any of the company's franchisees failed, and if so, for what reasons?
- Does the franchisor offer any flexibility regarding the products and services offered for sale?
- What is the term of the franchise agreement, and what is the fee for renewal?
- Are discounts available to franchisees who buy additional franchises?
- Are referral fees offered to franchisees who introduce the business to other prospective franchisees?
- What support does the franchisor offer in identifying suitable premises and remodelling the store?

Ask for a copy of the franchise agreement and the operations manual. Ask your lawyer to review the franchise agreement. Don't forget the agreement should always be equitable to each party; otherwise the franchise will not be successful.

Consider, also, the level of saturation in your targeted market. For example, in Thailand there are currently around 10,000 convenience stores. Of these stores, 7-Eleven has 3,750 outlets, Family Mart has 650, V-Shop has 800 and Freshmart has 300 stores. The deputy managing director of C.P. Seven-Eleven, a subsidiary of the Charoen Pokphand Group, claims that the market will be saturated when there are 20,000 convenience stores in the country. 7-Eleven will limit their outlets in Thailand to 5,000.

THE ADVANTAGES & DISADVANTAGES OF BUYING A FRANCHISE

The Benefits of buying a Franchise

If you want to go into business, but you lack the experience of business management or the type of business you want to venture into, why not consider buying a franchise?

A good franchise offers a complete business package including training, marketing, start-up, and operational procedures. Most franchisors do not require their franchisees to have previous experience of the business. Many successful franchisees have no business experience whatsoever, including civil servants, people who worked with the Armed Forces, and trades people. Franchisors are looking for motivated people with good communication skills from all backgrounds.

Business knowledge is an essential component of every successful business. Every good franchise has access to sound business knowledge and experience. The franchisee accesses this business knowledge via training and ongoing support offered by the franchisor.

Many franchises offer strong national branding which leads to familiarity of the franchise across the marketplace. The consumer is likely to trust the products offered by a franchise which has a strong brand name. This means that a new store within the franchise network can achieve much higher sales from the outset, compared with a business operated by a sole proprietor. It can take many years to build strong brand consciousness in a country, or internationally.

The key benefit to the potential franchisee is reduced risk of business failure. Statistics demonstrate that franchisees are much more likely to succeed in business than individual sole proprietors offering a similar service.

A good franchise is operating a proven business model. Any franchisee with sufficient motivation and reasonable communication skills should make a success of the franchise, unless they are particularly unlucky. The franchised business is controlled and monitored by the franchisor because the franchisor also has a vested interest in the success of all the franchisees.

Good franchisors will assist their franchisees in the following areas:

- Assistance with identifying a suitable location for the new store
- Support fitting and remodeling the new store

- Well known company name, logo and tag line
- Access to a successful product range
- Systematic and efficient procurement systems and stock control
- Training for new franchisees and their staff
- Operations manuals and business forms
- Accounting control systems
- Quality control procedures
- Promotional support at launch of the new store
- Joint advertising (and other marketing) at a national level
- Leads and referrals from the head office (or franchisor)

In addition to the above benefits, the franchise agreement may allow the franchisee to sell the business for a large profit in the future. Alternatively, the management or ownership may be taken over by the franchisee's sibling or other relation.

The Disadvantages of Buying a Franchise

Two key reasons for not buying a franchise are unsuitability of personality of the franchisee and the additional investment involved.

The cost of starting business as a franchisee is likely to be higher than starting in business independently. It may be worth the additional cost for the reduction in risk and the access to a turnkey operation.

Some people are not suitable franchisees: particularly anyone who insists upon making all the decisions. Franchises are controlled according to the operations manual and the franchise agreement. For example, the franchisor is unlikely to allow the sale of products outside the product line established by the franchise. Therefore it is necessary to conform to the standard procedures of the franchisor.

Occasionally, franchisees are resentful at having to pay large royalty fees to their franchisor when they have achieved success. They may feel that they (the franchisees) are doing all the work, and the franchisor is receiving a large share of their profits. However, the franchisee may never have achieved such success without the support of the franchisor in the first place.

The business relationship with the franchisor may turn sour. Therefore, it is essential to have an "exit strategy" which may involve selling the franchise back to the franchisor or to an outside party. Check the franchise agreement carefully, particularly with regard to any transfer fees payable to the franchisor on sale of the business. Usually, franchisors insist that all franchise owners are qualified and vetted by the franchisor, so any transferee would need approval by the franchisor.

Some franchisors may be difficult to work with; usually the same people take more from their franchisees than they are willing to offer by way of support. One disgruntled franchise licensee of a prominent business brokerage publicly bragged about how he cheated his franchisor out of numerous royalty commissions. After selling his franchise license a prospective buyer of the license reported the fraud to the franchisor. So check out your prospective franchisors and their associates carefully because the relationship is very important.

FRANCHISE CATEGORIES

Products

- Art Supplies & Frames
- Automobile: Truck Rental & Purchase
- Bath & Closet
- Beauty Salons, Supplies, Cosmetics & Modelling
- Books & Publications
- Clothing & Shoes
- Construction, Remodeling and Home Improvements
- Drug Stores
- Dry Cleaning & Laundry
- Equipment Rentals
- Fire Protection
- Floor-Related
- Florists and Plants
- Food: bakery, Bread & Doughnuts
- Food: Chicken Wings
- Food: Coffee & Tea
- Food: Grocery & Specialty Stores
- Food: Ice Cream, Yogurt, Smoothies, Candy, Popcorn & Beverages
- Food: Mexican
- Food: Pizza
- Food: Restaurant, Drive-in, Carryout & Delivery
- Food: Sandwiches, Subs & Salads
- Food: Sports Theme Restaurants
- Food: Steaks
- Furniture-Related
- General Merchandising Stores
- Gift Items
- Greeting Cards & Stationery
- Home-based Businesses
- Home Energy

- Home Furnishings & Decorating
- Home Furnishings: Windows & Treatments
- Home and Kitchen Items
- Jewelry
- Lawn & Garden Supplies & Services
- Martial Arts Related
- Hotels & Motels
- Optical Centers
- Party & Paper Goods
- Pet Centers & Pet-Related
- Photography
- Real Estate
- Retail (General)
- Security Systems
- Shipping, Packaging & Mail Centres
- Shoe Repair & Care
- Sports Equipment & Accessories
- Tools & Hardware Related
- Vending
- Video & Audio Products
- Vitamins & Supplements
- Water Conditioning & Treatment

Services

- Advertising & Direct Mail
- Accounting & Tax Services
- Auto Products & Services
- Business Aids & Services
- Children's Products, Education & Services
- Computer Sales & Services
- Concrete Services
- Consumer Buying Services
- Dating Services
- Educational Products & Services

- Employment & Personnel Services
- Environmental Products & Services
- Financial Services
- Franchise Attorneys
- Franchise Consultants
- Franchise Services
- Health Aids, Fitness Centers & Services
- Home Inspection Services
- Internet-Related
- Insurance
- Maid & Home Cleaning Services
- Maintenance & Cleaning
- Personalized Products & Services
- Printing & Copying Services
- Recreation & Entertainment
- Recycling Services
- Sign Products & Services
- Telecommunications Products & Services
- Travel Services
- Weight Control Centers

CONTENTS OF THE OPERATIONS MANUAL

The Operations Manual is the business blueprint which typically documents in detail the following aspects of the franchise:

- Shop layout
- Staff schedules
- Staff uniforms, appearance and etiquette
- Staffing requirements of outlets
- Job descriptions of staff
- Contracts of employment
- Disciplinary procedures

- Grievance procedures
- Training requirements
- Service standards
- Pricing policies
- Purchasing policies and standard form contracts
- Storage requirements
- Opening hours
- Stock rotation
- Accounting procedures
- Point of sale requirement
- Advertising and marketing practices
- Maintenance of equipment requirements
- Technical information about equipment used
- Cleaning routines
- Internal directory of franchisors organization
- Menus, recipes and variations
- Explanation of relevant laws
- Customer complaints procedures
- Guarantees and warranties
- Approved suppliers list

CASE STUDY

Typically the total investment required to establish a Subway franchise in Asia is US$115,000. The average monthly profit for such franchises is US$2,875, offering a 30% return on investment.

Subway offers franchisees a comprehensive start-up package including training and support. Franchisees are vetted for suitability prior to licensing.

The key to success is securing a prime location in a busy area and recruitment of a suitable business manager. Subway franchises provide a sophisticated inventory management system which highlights any possible theft. Inventory is checked weekly and any variances from budget are investigated. Theft by branch managers is limited by their POS (Payment on Sale) system and strict control over suppliers used. This enables franchisees to limit their involvement to supervision of the business, meaning that they do not require a work permit for the business.

For more information about Subway franchises, refer to the corporate website at www.subway.com or e-mail: franchise@subway.com.

FURTHER INFORMATION

If you are seriously considering ownership of a franchise attend one of the reputable franchise exhibitions and meet as many franchisors as possible. An international franchise exhibition calendar is available at the following website: **www.fdsfranchise.com/franchise-exhibition-calaendar**.

Useful franchise information is also available at the International Franchise Association website (www.franchise.org) and Franchise EK (www.franchiseek.com).

There are also several books and magazines which specialize in franchising, and these can be found on the above-mentioned websites.

123

CHAPTER 5: WORKING FREELANCE

If you have specialized skills and the ability to promote yourself, you should be able to earn a living anywhere in the world by working freelance.

Examples of portable skills include website programming, search engine optimization, graphic design, photography, jewelry design, astrology and spiritual consultancy, facilitating personal development workshops, teaching yoga, training and teaching, writing and editing.

Freelance practitioners usually charge their customers for their time on an hourly or daily basis. Customers normally reimburse any expenses incurred during the project. Sometimes practitioners charge their clients a flat percentage (typically 10%) of their fees to cover disbursements such as the cost of travel, printing and telephone calls.

The key advantages of working as a freelance practitioner are mobility, and start-up investment is nominal. Customers in "developed" countries do not need to know that their graphic designer is working from a tropical beach paradise where costs are low; however, expat freelancers are advised not to broadcast their chosen lifestyle, otherwise jealousy may harm the business relationship.

As a freelance practitioner, whenever you are not actually engaged with a client, you should be promoting and developing your skills, administering your business affairs or relaxing.

THE INVESTMENT

A major advantage of working freelance is that investment in the business is nominal. Website designers, graphic designers and writers need access to a computer with an internet connection. Photographers need suitable camera equipment.

The vocational or professional training courses are an essential part of your investment. Be aware that continuing professional education (CPE) is your ongoing responsibility to yourself and your clients. Keep up-to-date with the latest skills and technology otherwise you risk losing your clients. CPE includes membership of your professional or trade association, attending relevant seminars and reading appropriate books and technical digests.

Apart from computer hardware, freelancers usually need a mobile phone and a supply of business cards. If you have a reasonable internet connection you can speak to your customers using Skype (www.skype.com) at no cost. A replacement SIM card for your mobile phone and a box of business cards may cost less than US$20. Given the cost and importance of business cards, it's worth designing some impressive cards.

Many freelance practitioners develop their own website to promote their services. Websites are essential for practitioners selling to a worldwide marketplace. Itemize your services together with unique selling points, testimonials and a contact form. Promote your website and exchange links with online directories and businesses offering complementary services.

THE OFFICE

Freelancers enjoy the freedom of mobility and low overheads. Most people working freelance use a virtual office (or business website) and meet their clients in hotel lobbies, restaurants and cafés. It is not necessary to publish your residential address on your website or your business cards.

Some freelance website developers choose a comfortable internet café to use as their "office" during normal working hours. Working away from home tends to enhance emotional wellbeing and work output. Many cafés do not charge for Wifi access while others charge a nominal fee.

Identify a café offering Wifi using **www.wififinder.com**, **www.wififreespot.com** or **www.hotspothaven.com**.

WEBSITE & EMAIL ADDRESS

Most successful freelancers have a professional website which is promoted worldwide.

Choose a website domain name which describes your type of business. Use personalized mail forwarders from your USP to your personal email account.

Your website should contain pages about yourself, your services, testimonials, events, publications and a contact page. Use a contact form with email validation to prevent a barrage of spam in your email account.

The home page should summarize your service clearly and succinctly. Use photographs and other images to enhance the appearance of the site. Keep the text clear and concise, and sentences short. If you can spare the additional expense, ask your graphic designer to prepare a "mockup" of your home page for your website programmer.

List your website with as many appropriate online directories and search engines as possible. Some website owners exchange website links with appropriate businesses which are not in direct competition with each other.

NETWORKING

The key to success as a freelance practitioner is self-promotion and networking. Attend business and social events and mingle with potential customers. Always carry an adequate supply of business cards and exchange them whenever you meet a potential customer.

If you are a writer, attend launch parties for newly published books and chat with the publisher and author. If you are an artist or photographer, network with gallery owners and attend appropriate exhibitions. Freelance astrologers meet their clients in cafés and restaurants.

Carry with you a saleable product or brochure at all times. Self-published authors should always keep with them a copy of their latest book because willing buyers can appear anytime! The same applies to jewelry designers and other creative people.

Popular places for business networking include Chambers of Commerce, expat clubs, special interest groups and trade organizations. There are many international organizations with branches across the world such as Toastmasters (www.toastmasters.org), Rotary Club (www.rotary.org), Round Table (www.roundtable.co.uk/links.php) and The Hash Hound Harriers (www.gthhh.com) for "drinkers with a running problem."

Toastmasters, which provides a continuous training program for developing presentation skills, is a great organization for business networking. Rotary Clubs and Round Tables (or the 41 Club for those who are older) are excellent places for social and business networking, and fun.

Membership of an international trade association may allow contact with a local group overseas. For example, Skal Club (www.skal.org) represents professionals in the travel and tourism industry and Creative Circle represents designers and people working in the advertising industry.

Keep abreast of local events and "what's on," and attend events which may offer freelance business opportunities. Writers would normally benefit from networking with other authors and publishers at book launches and writers' clubs.

PROMOTION

Marketing your business is a creative process. Brainstorming with employees, family and friends tends to trigger good ideas. Never be complacent with your marketing formula because there is always scope for development.

Recommendation and referral by your satisfied clients is always the most effective marketing method. Not only do you need to provide a professional job, but your clients need to perceive your job as professional. Ask your clients for feedback and constantly act upon it to improve your service (and your clients' perception of your service).

Your most important promotional tool is your portfolio of successfully completed projects and positive testimonials received from your clients. If you are starting out as a freelance website designer, maybe you can provide a copy of your professional training certificate and the address of your own website.

Remember to ask each of your clients to complete a feedback form when you complete each assignment. Select appropriate positive comments for inclusion on your website's testimonials page.

Your marketing strategy starts with clearly identified "unique selling points" (USPs). USPs are product benefits or features giving your business an advantage over competitors. An example is *"The biggest sandwich in town"* or *"The quickest most efficient service."* Be clear about the edge you have over your competitors.

Here is a list of common ways to promote your business:

- Display advertising in magazines and newspapers
- Classified advertising in magazines, newspapers and internet
- Press releases, free advertorials in magazines, feature articles about your business in the local or specialist press
- Brochure distribution in public displays

- Gift marketing (including calendars, T-shirts and diaries)
- Corporate website and email marketing
- Business presentations and networking at expatriate and business clubs, such as Rotary Club and Chambers of Commerce.
- Networking at social clubs and trade associations
- Exhibitions, trade fairs and conferences
- Referral agreements and use of freelance agents
- Listings in authoritative guide books such as *Lonely Planet*

Referral agreements between complementary businesses which serve the same customers can be highly effective. For example a financial services consultant would benefit from a strategic alliance with a local lawyer. Both parties refer business to one another. Business associations of this kind only work if each party offers a different specialist service to a common targeted customer.

ADVERTISING

Display advertising in newspapers and magazines is usually expensive and often it is difficult to monitor the effectiveness of each advertising media. Businesses operating on very high gross profit margins tend to advertise widely in their marketplace, assuming that advertising generates sufficient sales to cover all associated marginal costs.

If you are thinking about advertising in a periodical it is necessary to know where the publication is distributed and who reads it. Many publishers do not provide demographic marketing data, but if possible, obtain the following information:

- Print-run (the total number of copies actually printed for each issue)
- Distribution (the number of copies physically distributed)
- Details of the distribution network
- Circulation and readership information
- Analysis of target readership
- Series discounts for repeating advertisements
- Introductory discounts (if applicable)
- Fee for graphic design of advertisement (if any)
- Free website link-exchange or free classifieds
- Free advertorial or a feature article about your new business

One common complaint by business people is that many free magazines are not distributed properly. Some publishers simply distribute their magazines to their advertisers (with a sales invoice attached). Some magazine publishers republish the same contents each month with a snazzy new cover.

If you host an event or launch a new service, send a press release to the local newspapers. Publishers do not charge for editorial. If you hold a business launch party be sure to invite the local press.

OFFSHORE CUSTOMERS

Keep in regular touch with your overseas customers. Some freelancers meet their American clients once a year during their family holiday. Usually they communicate with clients on a weekly basis by email, Skype or mobile phone.

Reliability, attention to details and deadlines are especially important for freelancers living overseas. Your choice of lifestyle should not be an issue with your clients as long as you meet their requirements and produce quality work on schedule.

ADMINISTRATION

Always ask new clients for a deposit in advance of at least 50% of the price quoted. The balance would become payable upon completion of the project.

Ask your customers to complete a feedback form or questionnaire when the project has been completed to their satisfaction.

Local customers usually pay by cash. Offshore customers usually prefer to pay in their home currency, directly into a bank account. An alternative payment method is online, using a payment gateway such as Paypal.com.

CASE STUDIES

Website Programming

Marco is an Italian website programmer living in Thailand. He purchased his own condominium for US$3,500, so his accommodation cost is limited to his electricity usage. He develops his own websites, which generate advertising income of around US$2,000 per month. He also offers website design services to both local businesses and overseas clients at a fee of US$50 per hour. Marco has lots of disposable income to play around with.

Teaching Yoga

Freelance yoga teachers usually promote themselves online with their own website. They also distribute brochures and A4-size posters in public places wherever their customers are likely to visit (typically at guesthouses, cafés, internet cafés, restaurants, massage schools and spas. Many freelance yoga teachers teach in several countries at natural health centers, so they publish their itinerary on their "schedule" page of their website.

CHAPTER 6:
ALTERNATIVE APPROACHES

There is no limit to the number of ways of earning a living overseas. The majority of expats earn a living in one of twelve ways which are listed in Chapter 7 (*Popular ways to Earn a Living*). In this chapter we will look at alternative ways of making a living.

You may have a great idea for a new business, but lack the necessary capital to fund the project. Alternatively you may have an interesting project proposal for a special expedition or other adventure.

Whatever you do, hold on to your vision and dreams, even if you don't have the financial backing yet. There are plenty of businesspeople and retirees with surplus funds awaiting adventurous, creative and talented people.

There are three main possibilities to consider:

- Seeking suitable investors to finance your business plan
- Seeking a suitable employer for the work you want to do
- Seeking sponsorship for your project by appropriate organizations

Your success in securing funding, employment or sponsorship depends upon a clear and focused proposal. The proposal should be marketed effectively to the appropriate people or organizations with enthusiasm. Enthusiasm is infectious, so your goal is to get your potential financiers excited about the project, and sell the concept to them.

SEEKING SUITABLE INVESTORS

You have a great business idea. If you don't have enough capital to fund the business, maybe you can find a willing partner to invest in your business. You can stipulate whether you want a working partner or a "non-executive" investor. It is usually more difficult sourcing a suitably skilled partner to work in the business.

A sound business plan is necessary before you present your proposal to potential investors. This document should answer most of the investors' questions. How much finance is required? What is the estimated return on investment? Include background information about you and your proposed management team.

The business plan is your roadmap to establishing a successful business. The document should include the following sections and information:

- Executive summary of the business
- Management team
- Profit forecasts
- Cash flow plan to support the application for funding
- Competition analysis
- Projected balance sheet with analysis of fixed and working capital
- Risk analysis
- Information for investors (including return on investment)
- Marketing plan
- Summary of unique selling points about the product or service

Refining the business plan is an ongoing task so get as much feedback about the document as possible.

The next stage is presentation of your plan to potential investors. Consider businesspeople who sell to a common customer base. Approach potential investors at local Chambers of Commerce, Toastmasters clubs, Rotary clubs, expat clubs and forums, and appropriate trade associations.

There are many retired people with bags of money, waiting for an interesting opportunity to add interest to their life. Some retirees have no family or commitments and would jump at the chance of being involved in an exciting new business project.

If business networking and targeted marketing does not yield the investment you need, place advertisements for investors in classifieds, newspapers and online notice boards.

SEEKING A SUITABLE EMPLOYER

Monitor the local classified advertisements for current recruitment opportunities and evidence of new businesses starting up in the local area. Freelance practitioners benefit from reviewing job advertisements because they provide information about new businesses starting up in the area which may require their expertise.

CASE STUDY: I noticed a business brokerage for sale among the local business classifieds. I made an appointment with the business owner to view the brokerage. While I was negotiating a price for the business, another buyer stepped in and paid the full asking price. The seller introduced me to the buyer and I was immediately offered a well-paid position as manager of the brokerage.

Some expat websites provide forums for jobs. Join these forums and post a notice about the job you are looking for.

SEEKING SPONSORSHIP FOR YOUR PROJECT

If you have an appetite for adventure and you really want to make things happen, why not seek sponsorship for your dream adventure? This option is limited only by your creativity and will to make it happen.

CASE STUDY: In May 2006 two English women started their 12,500 kilometer journey from Bangkok to England in a three wheeled vehicle (known as a *Tuk-tuk*). They completed the journey in 98 days, after driving an average of 127 Kilometers each day. The itinerary covered 11 countries (Thailand, Laos, China, Kazakhstan, Russia, Ukraine, Czech Republic, Germany, Belgium, France and England).

Jo and Antonia's above adventure was sponsored by several organizations and thousands of dollars were donated to a mental health charity in UK. Since completing the adventure, Jo and Antonia have written a book and the trip has been the subject of a documentary.

Every project begins with an idea or concept. Jo and Antonia's concept is summarized as "2 girls, 3 wheels, 19,200 kilometers; an epic overland adventure from Bangkok to Brighton in aid of MIND". MIND is a UK-registered mental health charity.

An expedition of this distance requires considerable planning and organization. Matters to consider include motor and medical insurance, documentation and procedures for temporary import of vehicles at country border crossings, driving licenses, spare parts for the tuk-tuk, media and sponsorship.

According to Wikipedia, the *Carnet de Passages en Douane* (CPD) allows drivers to temporarily import their vehicles without depositing a cash bond at the border. It is an international guarantee for payment of customs duties and taxes in case the vehicle is not re-exported from that country within the agreed period (which is usually 30 days). However, none of the countries through which Jo and Antonia traveled require the carnet.

A press release is necessary to interest the media including newspapers, travel magazines, online publishers, TV and radio stations. A press release is a one page project summary for the media. The girls also maintained a journal on their website together with photographs. The girls could be contacted by cell phone or by email.

Jo and Antonia managed to secure sponsorship from at least 18 organizations which were listed on their website. Some sponsors offered financial support while others supplied equipment or services for the expedition.

Sponsors want to see evidence of adequate media coverage. The underlying charitable cause is also a strong hook in sponsorship campaigns. Although sponsors usually write off their donations against taxable profits they expect positive publicity to help their organization.

HOUSE-SITTING

Now you can live rent-free anywhere in the world! If you are a freelance writer, website designer or artist, why not consider house-sitting overseas. House-sitting is one way of living in a comfortable home free of charge. There are several international house-sitting agencies listed with website search engines. One such agency is called House Carers (www.housecarers.com). Most agencies require house-sitters to pay a small annual membership fee for the service. The house owners list their house-sitting needs at no cost.

Here is an example of a recent house-sitting listing in Canada which was posted with Housecarers.com:

> We are looking for a mature, responsible housesitter for our home in the Pandosy Village area of the Mission in Kelowna in the Okanagan Valley for 7.5 months. Our home is on a very quiet street but close to shops and restaurants. It is also a very short walk to the Okanagan Lake and is within walking distance of downtown. For ski enthusiasts Big White is less than an hour's drive away. We have no pets.

Responsibility for payment of bills for electricity and other services is a matter for negotiation between you and the house owner.

CHRISTIAN ORGANIZATIONS

If you are a Christian there are many Christian organizations in America which may sponsor your trip overseas if you are willing to be a volunteer. There are many Christian organizations begging for volunteers worldwide.

CHAPTER 7:
POPULAR WAYS TO EARN A LIVING ABROAD

There are as many ways of earning a living abroad as there are stars in the sky. After living overseas for a few months you will learn many survival tricks and ways to make extra money. Expats tend to be resourceful people, and the experience of living abroad will support your ability to be creative and "think outside the box."

Be aware that it may be illegal to work without a work permit. Once you have a work permit you are in the Governmental system and expected to pay taxes. Furthermore it may be necessary to apply for business licenses to provide specific services. In some countries the bureaucracy can be intimidating.

Below is a list of the 12 most common ways for expats to earn a living:

- Employment with an international or foreign-owned company
- Teaching English as a foreign language
- Owning a local tourist-oriented business
- Real estate and business brokering
- Property development and management
- Online trading and auctions
- Freelance consulting of specialist services
- Writing and publishing
- Volunteering
- Website development
- Import/Export and manufacturing
- Online day trading of the financial markets

1. EMPLOYMENT WITH AN INTERNATIONAL OR FOREIGN-OWNED COMPANY

Although this option probably allows least freedom, it offers a good remuneration package enabling expats to live a comfortable lifestyle. Most employers regard overseas working experience with an international organization positively.

Professionals in the fields of banking, finance, law and consulting tend to find employment overseas easily because the large firms have an extensive network of offices worldwide. Internationally-recognized qualifications such as ACA (Associate member of the Institute of Chartered Accountants) enable qualified people to clinch overseas employment contracts.

Many international firms offer accommodation, return flights, health insurance and other benefits, as well as an attractive salary to employees posted overseas. The salary is usually comparable to the earnings in your home country, and therefore much higher than salaries offered by local firms.

If you are offered a lucrative position in paradise with an international firm, unless you have a valid reason for declining it, give it a try! In addition to the work experience and saving, you should have some fun and adventure too.

2. TEACHING ENGLISH

It is estimated that over one third of a billion people are studying English worldwide. If English is your mother language and you have a dynamic personality the world is your oyster. However many schools require teachers to possess a TEFL (Teaching English as a Foreign Language) certificate and a university degree. TEFL certificates are Diploma level.

Usually it is not necessary to speak the local language, though a working knowledge of the language will help with your job applications. Prospective teachers must have an understanding of the country's cultural issues, creativity and the ability to think "on their feet" and lots of patience.

The five main skills taught by English teachers are reading, writing, listening, speaking and thinking. The development of thinking skills is particularly important in cultures where learning is traditionally dogmatic and students learn by wrote.

If you don't have the ability or inclination to do an impersonation of a chimpanzee in front of 35 wide-eyed students, it may be wise to consider other options. The best teachers are good entertainers and communicators with a passion for education.

Entry criteria for teaching English vary from school to school. Two of the most prestigious English teaching certificates are the Cambridge Certificate in English Language Teaching to Adults (CELTA) and the Trinity TESOL certificate (Teaching English to Speakers of Other Languages). Both courses provide a rigorous training in teaching English during one month of fulltime study. A TEFL course from a recognized school can cost from US$500 to US$1,500, or more.

143

English for Specific Purposes (ESP) provides specialist English teaching programs for various professions such as business, medicine, banking, environmental economics and food technology. Business English is offered by many companies to develop practical business communication skills for direct application in the office. Typically students of Business English would learn how to write business letters, how to answer phone calls in the office, and how to table executive meetings.

CASE STUDY: Samantha specializes in English Specifically for Monks (ESM). She teaches monks in Northern Thailand how to train foreigners on Vipassana meditation retreats. Samantha wrote a course book for monks during her MA (TESOL) course at Payap University, Chiang Mai.

Many TEFL course providers have contracts with recruitment agencies or language schools overseas. Some schools guarantee a job for students who successfully complete their course.

There are numerous English teaching jobs listed on the internet such as www.daveseslcafe.com, www.tefl.com and www.ajarn.com. Most schools ask job applicants to email their resumé with a covering letter. Remember to scan your certificates and references; and keep an electronic copy. Most schools expect teachers to be dressed smartly in conservative attire.

Teaching opportunities are available in universities, government schools, international schools, language institutes and in companies. The most sought-after and prestigious jobs are offered by the international schools which usually require a degree in English, such as a bachelor of

Education (B.Ed.). Language institutes are commercial enterprises – either franchise chains or independent businesses - which tend to pay at lower rates.

Consider whether you want to teach children or adults. Children in Vietnam and Japan are much better behaved than in Thailand, where stronger leadership skills are necessary to maintain control of the classroom.

Although fulltime teachers typically teach 15-25 hours each week, it may be necessary to prepare lesson plans on site. Other schools are more flexible, allowing teachers to prepare for their classes at home. Fulltime teachers at Government schools usually work between 8.30am and 4.00pm. Language schools typically require their teachers to work between 5.00pm and 8.00pm on weekdays and daytime during the weekends.

If you do not want a fulltime teaching job, you may find private teaching work on a freelance basis (usually one to one). Some English language schools offer part-time teaching positions, but usually the pay is lower than for fulltime work. Some freelance teachers have no formal teaching credentials.

Many teachers in Thailand complain that their managers disallow them to fail their worst pupils. In Thailand all students are equal, though, as George Orwell said, *"Some are more equal than others."*

Teachers in Thailand are required by law to undergo cultural immersion training. Many schools provide their teaching staff with cultural training programs; whereas some schools demand that their foreign teachers arrange their own training without any financial assistance.

There are many teaching opportunities offered by the universities. Their entry criteria are a bachelor's degree (in any discipline) and professional appearance. Although pay rates are relatively low, employers typically offer annual teaching contracts with visa assistance and provision of a work permit. Part-time university teachers typically earn US$500 monthly, so other sources of income are usually necessary.

TEFL Certification

There are many TEFL training establishments in Southeast Asia. The most reputable schools in Thailand follow:

Chiang Mai University Language Institute (www.teflcmu.com)

The Language Institute of Chiang Mai University provides a 120 hour TEFL training program. The Language Institute also offers a one year training in the Thai language which enables students to obtain a one year education visa.

International House (www.ihbangkok.com)

International House provides the CELTA program in Thailand. The International House World Organisation (IHWO) is a network of 140 schools, teaching English to over 50,000 students in 47 countries. International House was founded in 1953 with the aim of providing an innovative approach to language teaching. International House Bangkok is Thailand's only affiliate member of IHWO. All IHWO teachers are Cambridge CELTA qualified. International House Bangkok also offers in-house business English tuition at company premises throughout Bangkok.

Payap University, Chiang Mai (www.payap.ac.th)

Payap University is a Christian educational foundation offering low cost TESOL (Teaching English to Students of Other Languages) training at certificate, advanced certificate and masters degree level. The master's degree in TESOL provides structured tuition over three semesters followed by thesis.

RECRUITMENT

Many TEFL training schools offer recruitment support to their graduates. The following websites offer job listings for English teachers:

- www.daveseslcafe.com
- www.ajarn.com
- www.transitionsabroad.com

Refer to the directory for contact information of universities and language schools. The most prestigious language schools include:

- AUA (www.auathailand.org)
- The British Council (www.britishcouncil.or.th)

The larger language schools, such as ECC, have branches throughout Thailand.

Recruiters

Newly-qualified and inexperienced English teachers occasionally benefit from the services provided by recruiters, especially when they start out in a new country.

147

Recruiters are sales-oriented commission hounds with a "duty of care" to their school principals. Recruiters are responsible for screening job applicants on behalf of the employer, and negotiating the teachers' remuneration package. The recruiter earns his or her fee once the teacher has worked beyond their probationary period (typically 3 to 6 months). Therefore recruiters are motivated to persuade their teachers to work beyond their probation, regardless of the teacher's experience.

A good recruiter helps expatriate teachers during their cultural immersion and relocation. Recruiters provide a support system for new arrivals from the moment they arrive at the foreign airport.

The expatriate teacher conducts all negotiations through their recruiter who acts as their agent. Usually recruiters provide country cultural orientation, guidance about language training, assistance with accommodation and lifestyle concerns. So recruiters benefit new expatriate teachers who need familiarization with a foreign country.

Once the initial contract has been served there is less benefit for teachers using a recruiter. Loyalty to a single recruiter ultimately stifles opportunities and freedom because they are motivated to urge their teachers to remain with the same employers.

CASE STUDY: Guidance by Les Elliott, Director of Studies of NAVA School of English

Teaching English demands different skills depending on the pupils being taught. However the two prerequisites of a good teacher in Thailand are attitude and the ability to have fun. *Mai sanook* means no fun, and if you hear these words in a classroom the teacher is in deep water regardless of age, experience, qualifications or skills acquired.

Attitude is everything. Thai teachers may appear lazy, disorganized and thirty years out-of-date regarding teaching techniques; but any foreign teacher who gets frustrated or criticizes the Thai teaching methods should leave. It is much easier to change yourself than it is to change others. This may sound defeatist but we have no right to change the Thais' approach. However if we provide great lessons for the students some of the more receptive Thai teachers will be influenced by our techniques.

A new foreign teacher usually earns three to four times as much as their Thai counterpart. Naturally this large disparity in remuneration sometimes causes resentment amongst Thai teachers; and some Thai teachers regard foreign teachers as an expensive novelty.

The key to successful teaching is acceptance. Say OK with a smile. Never react angrily in any situation. Try to adapt to every situation calmly with humor and patience.

Make the lessons fun. Your presence in the class must be dynamic. The students must be entertained. If you demand their attention, they will inevitably listen to you; and if they listen, they may learn. Even if they don't learn they are enjoying English with you. Students are the most reliable and vital evaluators of any teacher.

Evaluate your own personality before you start teaching in Thailand. Can you tolerate bizarre situations? Can you be a character in the class and maintain a high level of energy, even under stress? Tolerance and versatility will enable you to survive in the most challenging classroom environment.

Qualifications

The two essential qualifications for a teaching job in Thailand are a TEFL certificate and a degree in any discipline (from any University).

The TEFL course is straightforward but hard work, for three to six weeks. If you cannot apply yourself for the duration of the TEFL course then a career in teaching is probably the wrong path for you.

Most TEFL courses are invaluable. Some schools recruit teachers without a TEFL certificate because it isn't a requirement for a work permit in Thailand. TEFL training provides a strong foundation for the new teacher, and a real, albeit brief, experience of teaching. Graduates of the TEFL course also receive support and contacts for finding suitable employment. The schools that recruit teachers without a TEFL certificate expect lower quality staff and usually treat them with less respect and loyalty.

A university degree is prerequisite for a teacher's license in Thailand; and Thai Immigration provide work permits only to licensed teachers. Therefore anyone who wants to teach long term and legally in Thailand needs a university degree. Nowadays degree certificates are being scrutinized and transcripts are requested by employers. However, outside Bangkok fewer schools demand sight of university transcripts, despite their official recruitment policies. Some language schools recruit teachers without degrees for short periods because they are not eligible for a work permit.

Training

TEFL courses are available almost anywhere in the world. Most of the courses provide 120 hours of tuition over between four to six weeks. This may be the most valuable month for anyone wanting to teach long term. The TEFL course teaches classroom techniques, lesson planning, how to adapt lesson plans for varying levels of ability, and how to teach reading and pronunciation.

TEFL courses should provide real classroom experience. Teachers who want to teach in Thailand are advised to take their TEFL course in Thailand where they will meet Thai students. If teaching in Thailand is one of several options under consideration, you should **consider taking the course in your home country** because the course would have broader aims.

Approximately 80% of the teaching opportunities in Thailand are with children in schools. Few courses offer the opportunity to teach in a real school during their teaching practice. Despite the importance of the teaching practice most courses only provide six hours of actual classroom experience. Some full time teachers teach for six hours per day, which puts into perspective how 'tough' a TEFL course really is.

Check out the TEFL trainer. He or she should have several years of teaching experience in Thailand. Teaching in Thailand can be quite different to teaching in other countries. Although twenty years of teaching experience in Taiwan is useful, it's not as valuable as three years of teaching experience in Thailand for the trainee who wants to teach in Thailand.

151

CELTA (an acronym for Certificate in English Language Teaching to Adults) courses are recognized globally and they provide a thorough foundation for teaching adults. Successful CELTA trainees are well prepared for any English class. However they are specifically aimed at teaching adults, but most teaching in Thailand is with children. However, most CELTA graduates manage to adapt their skills to work with younger students.

A major benefit of TEFL training is the opportunity to get practical experience in a supportive environment. Flexibility - the ability to adapt easily and quickly - is essential. The first few months of teaching experience is about learning effective classroom management techniques with students of varying ability.

The TEFL training providers in Thailand are regulated by the Thai Ministry of Education (www.moe.go.th).

Employment Options

Employment options are plentiful, so with a little persistence you should be able to secure enough work anywhere. However the work may not be too satisfying initially. Some teachers manage to clinch plum jobs with excellent pay straight away. Don't expect to be offered an amazing job at the beginning of your career; be realistic.

The least coveted teaching positions are freelance (Do-it-yourself). Display a few posters written in Thai with your name and phone number in areas frequented by students. Once the calls start coming in, arrange to meet, perhaps in a coffee shop. Use an English workbook to facilitate and structure your lessons. After the introductory lesson make sure the student pays in advance for at least six lessons

POPULAR WAYS TO EARN A LIVING ABROAD

because many students cancel at the last minute. Freelance teaching is an insecure option.

Many teachers start out by applying to as many language schools as possible. Usually they will take just one teaching position offering many hours of work. Most of the schools' students pay for a set number of hours of one-to-one or classroom tuition. Once these hours have expired there is no certainty they will continue. It is possible to secure a reasonable living by working for several language schools consecutively.

The disadvantage of working for language schools is that classes are held during evenings and weekends. Also these positions do not provide work permits so they are not legal long-term options. Language schools offer excellent short term experience that will appeal to the more prestigious schools later. Talk to other teachers and ask for work teaching a variety of class sizes and ages of students. This way you identify your favorite style.

If you are available in the summer months of March and April there are summer schools across Thailand. Summer schools are usually hard work but lots of fun. Since they are like holiday camps most employers prefer younger teachers with a flair for 'edutainment'.

Most teaching jobs in Thailand are in schools. The schools are split into three categories: Kindergarten, Primary and Secondary schools.

Kindergarten, which is called Anubaan, lasts for three years; primary school, known as Prathom, lasts for six years; and secondary school, which is called Mathyom, is also for six years.

Students are required by law to study for nine years from prathom 1 to mathyom 3, but in the cities the vast majority study for all fifteen years. Usually foreign teachers are required to teach general conversation and the more demanding 'English Programs'. General conversation teachers usually teach many different classes each week. If a teacher has five different classes at the same age level, they can use the same lesson plans and therefore save on pre-class preparation. The students can be inattentive, lazy or unable to understand even the simplest vocabulary or phrases. Many of these students are fun too.

English is of little interest to many students, so it's essential to make the classes fun. English programs are very different. There are several ways for Thai students to study English intensively now; and many schools require students to study science, mathematics and social studies in English. The teacher benefits by getting to know their students well because they probably teach the same people every day. The disadvantage is that each lesson is taught only once so each lesson requires preplanning. A background in the subject being taught is an obvious advantage. The older students tend to be more difficult to teach.

There are also teaching jobs available in colleges and universities, but they are far fewer in number and suited more to experienced teachers. If a course is taught in English then students have a much greater understanding of grammar. If you are up for this challenge it can be most rewarding. For many courses though, English is a minor requirement and the students are well below the required standard.

For further information about teaching English at NAVA School, contact Les Elliott. Tel: +66 (0)53 222 177 or internet: www.navaschool.com.

3. OWNING A LOCAL TOURIST-ORIENTED BUSINESS

If you have enough money to purchase a business, and you enjoy working with people, why not start your own guesthouse, hotel, restaurant, bar, or internet café?

Research the popular tourist destinations which coincide with your idea of paradise. The most fashionable and developed tourist locations are most expensive. For example, buying a business in Thailand's beach resort of Phuket would require more capital than in northern Thailand.

Establish an investment budget before actively looking for a business. There are many ways to find a suitable business – from networking to using business brokers and checking the business classifieds – and these are covered in Chapter 3 *(Buying an Independent Business)*.

Buyer Beware! (Caveat Emptor). It is the buyer's responsibility to validate all representations provided by either seller or the seller's broker. Chapter 3 offers advice on how to check the seller's financial information and how to value the business. Do not make an offer until your due diligence is complete.

To view businesses for sale around the world, refer to the Sunbelt Network website at www.sunbeltnetwork.com.

4. REAL ESTATE AND BUSINESS BROKERING

In many countries real estate and business brokering is unregulated. This means that no training or qualifications are necessary for property intermediaries. Furthermore many people offer real estate agency services on a part-time basis alongside other activities.

Freelance real estate brokers can earn relatively large commissions without much investment of time or money. It is possible to earn commissions on a freelance basis if you are good at networking.

Here are the steps you must follow to earn your agency commissions:

- Identify some properties for sale and obtain an agency agreement with the owner
- Network with potential property buyers or advertise in the local classifieds
- Keep close contact with the potential buyer at all times and assist with the negotiations between buyer and seller
- Collect your commission from the seller as soon as the property has been transferred to the buyer

Real estate agency is popular in many prime tourist locations such as Bangkok, Pattaya and Phuket in Thailand where property brokering is unregulated. Suitable locations attract retirees and regular visitors for their holidays. Choose a location that is booming, where property prices are rising or an area where tourism is undergoing development such as Sihanoukville in Cambodia.

Most expatriate brokers target buyer who live in American, Europe or Australasia. Prospective buyers are in the local bars and restaurants or relaxing on golf courses and beaches. The hottest prospects are aged 40s to 60s and either semi or fully retired.

Always get the seller's agreement to pay your commission in writing. A signed agreement is ideal, though agreement by email usually suffices for freelance agents.

Identify private property developers other owners of real estate in the local classified newspapers or online listings. View and photograph the properties for sale and collect the owners' contact information (email address and mobile number). When you have found a prospective buyer, tell the seller and ask him to confirm his agreement to pay your commission for introducing the buyer.

CASE STUDY: I noticed an advertisement for the sale of a condominium in Phuket for US$105,000. I viewed the property. A few weeks later a colleague told me about a visitor wanting to buy such a condominium. I emailed details of the property to him (without information about the seller). The visitor was interested, so I asked the buyer to confirm his agreement to pay me the standard agency commission of 3% if I introduce a buyer. The seller immediately confirmed by email. Afterwards the buyer made an offer of US$95,000 and the deal closed at the same price. Within 2 hours of completion the seller paid me my commission of US$2,850 in cash. It really was that easy! All I needed was an internet address and a mobile phone.

If you want to work fulltime in business or real estate agency you need capital to pay for your office rent, vehicle, secretary-cum-receptionist, local listing agents and sales negotiators. Most real estate agents need to advertise extensively in local periodicals. You will need to license your business, obtain a work permit and pay the local taxes.

For further information about business brokering, check out *The Complete Guide to Business Brokerage* by Tom West, published by Business Brokerage Press (www.businessbookpress.com). Also look at the website of Sunbelt Business Advisors (www.sunbeltnetwork.com), the largest franchisor of business brokerages.

If you choose to start a real estate agency consider joining a worldwide real estate network such as NAI Global (www.naidirect.com). Member organizations receive quality enquiries and pay royalties on fees earned. There are several international real estate franchisors listed with the International Franchise Association (www.franchise.org). Some real estate businesses offer professional training courses for real estate professionals such as First National Real Estate.

5. PROPERTY DEVELOPMENT AND MANAGEMENT

I have met several foreign property developers in Asia who have profited from the growing demand for refurbished condominiums. The developers pay nominal tax on their profits, usually a proportion of the fees levied by the land registry when the property is transferred.

Foreign ownership of land is restricted in many developing countries to protect the country from being taken over. Usually foreigners are allowed to purchase condominiums if the majority of the units are locally owned. Check the local laws concerning foreign ownership of property before investing.

The most popular opportunities for property developers are in the up-and-coming tourist locations which attract holiday makers and retirees from around the world. Many businesspeople and retirees want to own their own home or apartment which has been built to western standards.

The most successful property developers buy blocks of repossessed condominium units from banks at auction. Typically they may pay US$7,000 per unit for a lot of ten units in the same building. The developers usually employ a team of semi-skilled employees permanently for building and painting work.

The cost of renovation, refurbishment and furnishing to western standards may double their investment to US$14,000 per unit. They sell the refurbished units from US$20,000 to US$30,000+.

The major challenge for property developers is controlling the quality of the workmanship and constantly juggling finances to keep the workforce occupied. Your reliable local foreman should be paid on a performance basis with penalties for poor workmanship or delays.

Try to maintain control over all purchases of materials otherwise your local foreman or contractors may receive substantial commissions – or kickbacks – from your suppliers.

Always pay your contractors progressively for work done. Never pay your contractors in advance otherwise you will lose control of the project.

There are benefits of using bank finance for your property development project other than restricting financial transfers from overseas. Usually the bank monitors the progress of the construction and identifies any defective workmanship.

6. ONLINE TRADING AND AUCTIONS

Online trading platforms, such as Ebay.com, enable thousands of people to live and work in exotic countries around the world. Online trading is one of the world's fastest-growing businesses. Products for sale in Europe and America are usually between 5 and 10 times more expensive than those in developing countries. Online traders take advantage of these price differentials, enabling them to live a comfortable life in paradise.

Many expats selling Asian products to a worldwide marketplace via the internet claim monthly profits of between US$1,000 and US$2,000. Successful online trading depends upon the uniqueness of your product and how it is presented. Some auction websites have many traders competing for the same buyers, while others favor the traders.

Products which sell for a high price are either unique or fashionable. Popular brand names are easy to sell, though the major auction websites try to prevent infringement of copyright or patents. In Asian markets counterfeit goods are common. The major online auction sites, such as **www.ebay.com**, close down trading accounts if they suspect illegal trading activity.

Many online traders residing throughout Asia do not have work permits, which is why it is important to have a local partner as manager and representative. Instead of working, they are investors and overseers. Traders usually declare a Post Office address (or PO Box number) as the sender's address on the package.

POPULAR WAYS TO EARN A LIVING ABROAD

The low cost of investment to start up this business is an obvious attraction. The prerequisites for online trading include a computer with internet connection, use of a digital camera, and an online bank account in the country of the online trading platform.

Registration with a suitable online trading platform takes a few minutes. Setting up an account with the Paypal (**www.paypal.com**) payment gateway is optional. Many buyers prefer to pay by direct bank credit using either telephone or internet banking. It will be necessary to check your online bank account daily to confirm your orders pending delivery.

Popular products for sale include fashion accessories, silver jewelry, belt buckles, shirts, handbags and cds. Traders usually start with 50 or more auctions running consecutively. Some traders get assistance to negotiate low prices for goods at the local markets. Typically 50 T-shirts which cost US$2.25 each (total: US$112.50) and sell for over US$12 each (total: US$600). This example represents a profit of 433%.

Your business terms and conditions should request buyers to wait up to two weeks for delivery. Your customer should receive their goods in less time than expected. It also helps to offer a "no quibble money back guarantee" if they return the goods in good condition within say 2 weeks. Don't forget the importance of establishing a sound trading (customer feedback) history. Negative feedback by customers will harm your business, so keep your customers satisfied.

Products which are identified as based in Asia are much more difficult to sell compared to items stored in Europe

161

or America. Many online traders respond to this issue by declaring their products for sale in their home country, with a proviso in their Terms & Conditions that products may be delivered from USA (for example) or Asia.

Many auction websites allow trading free of charge. Ebay.com and some of the more established internet platforms charge a small percentage of the sale price. Beware of fixed fees which apply regardless of whether the product sells or not.

Choose light items because postage can be relatively expensive, although you charge for postage & packing. Jewelry, cds, handbags, belt buckles and T-shirts are the most popular goods traded because they are light and widely marketable. Traders usually charge the standard postal rates for their home country, though some add a premium to their P & P fee.

The more experienced and sophisticated traders invest in product displays and elegant backdrops to enhance the presentation of their goods. Another avenue for experienced traders is formation of an online store, selling their products at fixed prices.

Christmas is the best time to take a holiday because the postal system operates at full capacity and delivery is much slower. Customer satisfaction is critically important because an unfettered track record will help you attract more customers.

7. FREELANCE CONSULTING OF SPECIALIST SERVICES

If you provide specialist skills and you want to work freelance in paradise, refer to chapter 5 (*Working Freelance*).

Your capital investment is likely to be limited to the cost of a computer notebook, a box of business cards and a mobile phone. The freelance practitioner meets clients in comfortable hotel lobbies, restaurants and cafés, according to the client's lifestyle.

There are many American website programmers living and working freelance in Asia. Many of these freelancers earn standard business rates from their American customers while their local cost of living is below one quarter of what they would spend in USA.

There is also a local market of businesspeople requiring computer services including website design and promotion. However most freelancers are so busy servicing the needs of their overseas customers, they don't need to accept contracts locally.

One Belgian freelance website developer commented that most of his European clients have no idea that he is "working" from tropical paradise. He also mentioned that he tries to keep a secret of his whereabouts; otherwise his clients may become envious and ask for lower consultancy rates.

8. WRITING & PUBLISHING

If you enjoy writing there are many ways to make a living from this skill. The emergence of the worldwide web has increased the opportunities for budding scribblers.

Travel Writing

Travel writing is a popular occupation as there are a growing number of travel websites and magazine publishers wanting interesting articles about travel adventures. Some writers specialize in stories aimed at expats, while others write guidebooks on subjects ranging from building a house to day trading in paradise.

Publishing Proposals & Queries

Fiction writers usually complete their manuscript before submitting "queries" to publishers. Writers of nonfiction tend to send queries to publishers during the early stages of the project. A query is a one page "attention-grabber" and summary of the publishing concept, including the author's biodata and contact information. If the publishers are hooked by your query they would usually request a more detailed publication proposal which includes competition analysis and proposed marketing information.

Writers increasingly need business management skills. Ability to write articulately is prerequisite. Publishers are looking for commercially-oriented writers with an irresistible concept supported by a sound marketing strategy. Too many wannabe writers focus on subjects satisfying themselves but not necessarily the marketplace of readers.

Literary Agents

Literary agents act as a bridge between author and publisher. Literary agents typically charge the author 10%-15% of the gross royalties payable to the author. A professional agent will present your work to suitable publishers. The publishing industry is "old school" and relationships are the key to success. Literary agents usually open more doors for authors and help maximize worldwide royalty income.

Timeline

If you propose to write a book for a publishing house, allow 12 months from acceptance of your proposal through to publication date. The editorial process may take between two weeks and three months. The cover design and layout of the "guts" of the book may take several weeks to complete. All text requires proofreading and checking in detail.

Writers' Resources

The Writer's Handbook, published by MacMillan, is a useful guide for authors. The guidebook contains listings of publishers and literary agents in USA, UK and other countries. Other essential resources include WritersMarket.com (also available in print each year) and WritersDigest.com. The Writer's Market publication contains 3,500+ listings of publishers, trade journals and literary agents.

Magazine Publishing

Some expats choose to start up their own magazines, usually supported by local advertisers. However many magazine publishers discover that their main business is actually selling advertising.

If you have well-developed writing or editorial skills you should be able to find a job with a local newspaper or magazine publisher in many countries. Although a recognized training in journalism and media would be preferred, it is by no means mandatory. There is a shortage of professional editors.

Writers' Clubs

There are writers' clubs and interest groups in many expat centers around the world. These groups can offer a useful support network together with exchange of ideas and contacts. Writing can be a lonely occupation, so interaction with other wordsmiths can be fun while offering professional development.

Vanity Publishing

Do not throw money at vanity publishers who promise to publish your book at considerable cost to the author. If you cannot clinch a deal with a suitable publisher, you may benefit from publishing your book independently (or self-publishing). Typically a 200 page book may cost US$2.50 - US$4.00 to design and print overseas. Your book distributor will charge between 40% and 60% of the cover price.

CASE STUDY: Bob lives in Pattaya. He self-published a nonfiction book and contracted with a local book distributor to sell his books to a countrywide chain of bookshops. He printed 2,000 copies and sold 1,000 copies within 12 months of publication. The recommended retail price of the book is US$10.00. The distributor charges 40% (including retail discount). The cost of designing and printing all 2,000 books was US$1,500, so Bob's net profit for the first year was US$4,500. He expects to sell the remaining 1,000 books over the next 18 months, making an additional net profit of US$4,500. Therefore Bob expects a return of US$9,000 on his investment of US$1,500.

Electronic Publishing

Do consider publishing your work on the internet with an e-book publisher. Escapeartist.com is one example of many online publishers. Online publishers give a larger percentage of the cover price to the writers because the cost of production and distribution is much lower than with traditional print publishing.

The ten steps to getting published are:

1. Concept - summary
2. Title – brainstorm and get feedback; use group feedback (eg writers' group)
3. Check competing titles eg search on Barnes & Nobles (www.bn.com)
4. Note the main specialist publishers for this subject area
5. Consider which level of publisher you are targeting (large, medium or small)
6. Prepare the query letter on 1 page A4
7. Summarize your USPs – reasons why the market will PREFER YOUR BOOK
8. Prepare a full length publishing proposal
9. Prepare the shortlist of all suitable publishers to whom you will submit the query letter
10. Refer to the publishers websites for submission guidelines and follow the instructions carefully

CASE STUDY: I attended the book launch party of Mo Tejani's *Chameleon's Tales* at Chiang Mai's Writer's Bar. At the party I met the director and owner of Mo's publisher, Paiboon Publishing. Shortly afterwards, I was asked to write a business guide book for Thailand. Such is the effectiveness of social networking. The following year I hosted my own launch party for *How to Establish a Successful Business in Thailand* at the same venue.

Further Information

If you are seriously interested in freelance travel writing you must obtain a copy of Lonely Planet's book called *Travel Writing* by Don George (ISBN: 0-8644-2742-5).

Further information about publishing of non-fiction in Southeast Asia is available at **Fasttrackpublishing.com**. Alternatively contact Philip Wylie via email (**Philip@philipwylie.com**).

9. VOLUNTEERING

People of all ages, backgrounds, income levels, and abilities spend between two weeks and three years volunteering in different capacities on projects all over the world. You could volunteer on almost any type of project imaginable. Here are some examples of projects you could volunteer on:

- Constructing a school or clinic
- Promoting healthcare in rural villages
- Working with a women's cooperative
- Practicing sustainable agriculture
- Teaching English

- Protecting sea turtle habitat
- Joining an archeological dig
- Helping renovate a castle or monastery
- Developing small business enterprise
- Supporting human rights efforts

The guidebook entitled *How To Live Your Dream of Volunteering Overseas* provides information about volunteering in a user-friendly format featuring quotes, worksheets, case studies, and inspiring stories. The book is based on six years of research that included fieldwork in over 25 countries, the book is not just a directory of opportunities, but a critical review of over 80 volunteer placement organizations in this rapidly growing field, as well as a detailed but easy to read manual about everything from why to volunteer to what to do when you get back. *How To Live Your Dream of Volunteering Overseas* is an in-depth guide for anyone who wants volunteer in Latin America, Africa, Asia, the Middle East or Eastern Europe. The book may be purchased from the following website: *www.volunteeroverseas.org*.

The Cost of Volunteering

Most programs offering international volunteer opportunities charge volunteers a fee to cover their administration and operational costs. Many of the voluntary organizations need to raise funds to contribute materials and other essential resources to the overseas project. Host communities do not usually have sufficient resources to accommodate and feed volunteers, and if they had money to pay volunteers, they would probably hire a local person who speaks the language and understands the culture. However there are a few international volunteer programs such as the Peace Corps and International Executive Service Corps which cover the cost of your room, board, and airfare. In most other cases, part of volunteering abroad means a commitment to fundraising.

Further Information

The International Volunteer Programs Association (IVPA) is an alliance of nonprofit, non-governmental organizations that are involved in international volunteer and internship exchanges. IVPA's website is: **www.volunteerinternational.org**

The Peace Corps is one of the largest organizations supporting volunteers. The website is **www.peacecorps.gov**.

Other useful resources for anyone considering volunteering abroad are:

- Transitions Abroad (www.transitionsabroad.com)
- Volunteer Abroad (www.volunteerabroad.com)

10. WEBSITE DEVELOPMENT

You can develop and publish websites almost anywhere in the world. So why not develop websites in paradise where you can enjoy a high quality of life? Although you will have low living costs, you will earn dollars or euros from your e-commerce projects.

If you have the necessary technical or management skills, this type of business can be operated from anywhere with a reasonable internet connection.

There are basically two types of website project:

- Content-based internet site
- E-commerce internet site

The Content-based Internet Site

This type of website gives away free information about a specific interest (eg information about a city or country). The website owners' objectives are to offer as much comprehensive reliable information for their target audience and to promote the website effectively.

The success of the website depends upon the number of visits to the site. The business receives an income from advertisers. The most popular form of adverting relates to Google's *Adsense* (www.google.com/adsense/). If your website is promoted well and you are highly ranked on the internet search engines, Google may allow you to participate on the Adsense programme.

How *Adsense* works: You allow Google to promote Google's advertisers on your website. For each referral you direct to Google's advertisers, you receive income. Google's advertisers pay fees to Google according to the number of visits (or clicks) directed to their website via third party website owners. .

Success in the business increases as website content (ie the number of web pages) increases. The website development is a continuous process, expanding and refining all the time. The website must be promoted well. It should be listed on as many internet directories as possible. Also, the website should contain embedded meta-tags containing the heading and keywords relevant to your site. Another method of website marketing is by way of link exchange (a mutual linking of websites).

E-Commerce Website

E-commerce websites are used to sell specific products and services. Most e-commerce websites use a "shopping cart" software program. These websites require a payment gateway enabling electronic payment by customers. The most common and easy to use payment gateway is Paypal (www.paypal.com). Paypal accepts payment via credit cards (eg Visa and Mastercard) and allows the merchant to withdraw the receipts.

The e-commerce website business can be much more complex than the aforementioned information-based website; particularly when warehousing and distribution are involved as well as maintaining the electronic payment system. The promotion of the e-commerce website is equally as important as the information-based website. But an e-commerce website may generate hundreds of customers; whereas the information- based website only needs one contract – with Google.com.

What Makes An Effective Website

Every website contains the following components:

- The domain name registration and e-mail forwarding
- Graphic design of the website
- Website programming of the basic functions (including databases, links, contact forms and payment gateways)
- Website hosting
- Website promotion

Each of these four components is important. Probably the biggest mistake is to overspend on website design and underestimating the importance of website promotion. Establish a realistic budget for promotion. What is the point of developing a sophisticated website that nobody visits?

Domain Name Registration and E-mail Forwarding

The location of your domain server is unimportant. It is beneficial to use the same company for both domain hosting and domain registration. You should have personal access to a password-protected control panel, enabling you to upload your website at any time. The cost of domain name registration and e-mail forwarding starts from US$20 per annum.

The name of your website should express the nature of the business. Therefore, a good name for an information-based website for expats is www.expat.com.

It always looks more professional to promote your email address when it contains your unique domain name, instead of a hotmail address. It is easy to arrange e-mail forwarding to your personal e-mail account (eg from philip@philipwylie.com to a personal email address.

Website Design

There are many skilled website programmers scattered around the globe, but many of them lack graphic design skills. The rates charged by website designers in paradise can be a fraction of the fees charged by US and European designers. The cost of building an information-based website is usually much lower than for e-commerce websites.

173

Good planning and preparation prior to requesting quotations for design can save a lot of your money. Work out how many web pages you need and how you want them linked together. Identify a good website on which to model your project. Consider listing the main classifications and sub-classifications on an Excel spreadsheet. The optimal number of words per web page is 300, so work out how many pages you need. Decide which fonts to use and what images to include.

When you approach website designers for quotations, ask them for website addresses of projects they have completed for their clients. Evaluate their work. Is it well constructed? Are there any spelling mistakes? Is it laid out properly? Is it user friendly? Try a Google search to discover the website's raking using a suitable keyword (if the designer is also responsible for its promotion). Check that they can do all the work themselves, because some practitioners need to subcontract graphic design or database design.

The best way to identify good website designers is to source the best websites owned by businesses in your area. Find out who has the best website and then source the designer. Alternatively, check the private advertisements of website designers. Usually website designers can be found tapping their notebooks in comfortable cafés (which offer internet access), as they sip their latte or nibble their almond slice.

Website Hosting

Website hosting requires a server with sufficient memory for your website program. Hosting packages vary in price according to the size and complexity of the website.

Small home-based website hosting plans usually start at US$5+ per month; corporate website hosting plans are more expensive. Some hosts interrupt the internet connection during routine computer maintenance.

Website Promotion

Website promotion demands work at set-up (when the website is designed) and ongoing marketing services. Establish a quarterly budget for website promotion because the task of maintaining a high ranking with internet search engines is continuous.

There are certain steps which must be taken when the website is designed. The site must convey clearly the purpose of the site. Your domain name should be congruent with the objectives of your website. Meta-tags containing page title and keywords must be embedded in the programming of each web page; this enables internet search engines to identify your website.

Your website designer may also incorporate a link exchange system. You promote an associate's website and they promote yours. This two-way referral system works well between businesses which complement each other, rather than competing businesses.

Get listed on as many website directories as possible; sometimes registration is free but some companies charge an annual fee. Many established websites allow banner advertising but this may be expensive. If you are considering advertising with a website, check their ranking using relevant keywords on the major search engines.

Offering a free weekly or monthly e-newsletter is a great marketing tool which enables you to build up a mailing list. The newsletter reminds your target audience about your website. People forward these e-newsletters to their friends if they are impressed.

Online Trading

Online trading platforms, such as Ebay.com, enable thousands of people to live and work in exotic countries across Southeast Asia. Online trading is one of the fastest-growing businesses in the world. Products for sale in Europe and America tend to be at least five times more expensive than the equivalent items in Thailand. The price difference enables online traders to live freely away from the oppressive regulations imposed by developed countries.

Most of the anonymous online traders interviewed claim to earn US$1,000-2,000 each month. Success in online auctions depends upon the following factors:

- Marketability of your product
- Presentation of the product (including photograph and description)
- Competition by other traders
- The online trading platform chosen
- Your opening offer price and terms of business
- Customer feedback (or track record)

Products which sell for a good profit are either unique or fashionable. Popular brand names are easy to sell. In Asia many items for sale in the markets are counterfeit. Selling copies of branded products infringes copyright law. The major online auction sites, such as Ebay.com, close down trading accounts if they suspect illegal trading activity.

Many online traders residing throughout Asia do not have work permits, which is why it's important to have a local partner as manager and representative. Technically they are investors and overseers. Usually they declare a Post Office address as the sender's address on the package.

The relatively low cost of investment to start this business is an obvious incentive. The prerequisite conditions for online trading are:

- A computer with an internet connection
- Use of a digital camera
- An internet bank account in the country of the online trading platform
- An inventory of products for sale

Registration with a suitable online trading platform takes a few minutes. Setting up an account with the Paypal (www.paypal.com) payment gateway is optional. Many buyers prefer to pay by direct bank credit using either telephone or internet banking. It will be necessary to check your online bank account daily to confirm your orders pending delivery.

Popular products for sale include fashion accessories, silver jewellery, belt buckles, shirts, handbags and cds. Traders usually start with 50 or more auctions running consecutively. Some traders get assistance from a local friend to negotiate low prices for goods at the local markets. Typically, 50 T-shirts might cost US$2 each and sell for over 9 Euros each (usually over US$700 in total).

Your business terms and conditions should request buyers to wait up to ten days for delivery. It's important that your customer receives their goods in less time than expected. It also helps to offer a "no quibble money back guarantee" if they return the goods in good condition within say 2 weeks. Don't forget the importance of establishing a sound trading (customer feedback) history. Negative feedback by customers will impede your business, so keep your customers satisfied.

Products which are identified as based in Asia are much more difficult to sell compared to items stored in Europe or America. Many online traders respond to this issue by declaring their products for sale are based in their home country, with a proviso in their *Terms & Conditions* that products may be delivered from UK (for example) or Asia.

Many auction websites allow trading free of charge. Ebay.com and some of the more established internet platforms charge a small percentage of the sale price. Beware of fixed fees which apply regardless of whether the item sells or not.

Choose light items because postage from Thailand is relatively expensive, although you charge for postage & packing. Jewellery and T-shirts are the most popular goods traded because they are light and widely marketable. Traders usually charge the standard postal rates for their home country, though some add a premium to their P & P fee.

The more experienced and sophisticated traders invest in product displays and elegant backdrops to enhance the presentation of their goods. Another avenue for experienced traders is formation of an online store, selling their products at fixed prices usually.

Christmas is the best time to take a holiday because the postal system operates at full capacity and delivery is much slower. Customer satisfaction is critically important because an unfettered track record will help you attract more customers.

For information about search engine optimization, check out **Virtualtravelguides.com**.

11. IMPORT/EXPORT AND MANUFACTURING

If you are planning to establish a factory or import / export business overseas, your embassy's commercial attaché may be able to offer guidance and useful contacts. Membership of your local chamber of commerce is another prime source of business information. To identify your nearest chamber refer to the World Chambers website at: **www.worldchambers.com**.

Many countries offer extensive support to foreign businesses. Examples of support include export promotion centers, economic free zones for investors, tax incentives and subsidized rent and services. Most developing countries provide a Board of Investment to assist and promote foreign investment.

Your three main options are:

- Exporting locally-manufactured products
- Manufacturing and exporting products from paradise
- Importing and marketing of products in paradise.

The key issue for most manufacturers and exporters in developing countries is quality control. Establish a sound quality control management system. What's the point of manufacturing thousands of cheap products if they are rejected or otherwise obsolete?

Popular products for export include jewelry, gemstones, clothes, handicrafts and leather products. Typically these products sell in America for over ten times the purchase price.

Gemstones and jewelry are favored due to the relatively low cost of delivery.

Favorable locations for exporters are influenced by exchange rates, productivity of local labor, wage rates, cost of transportation and bureaucracy. Currently China, Vietnam and India are popular countries for exporters.

Check the country's list of prohibited imports and exports before researching the import or export duties. Export duties are payable to the Customs Department before shipping is permitted. The lists of import and export tariffs, which can be very detailed, are published by each country's Customs Department.

Freight forwarders usually provide exporters with a one-stop transportation service which includes assistance with customs and shipping documentation, insurance and packing. Transportation is either CIF (Cost, Insurance and Freight) or FOB (Free on Board). Importers contracting on CIF terms are responsible for the goods from the port of arrival; whereas importers buying on FOB terms are responsible for the goods as soon as they are loaded onto the sea vessel.

12. ONLINE DAY TRADING OF THE FINANCIAL MARKETS

There are a growing number of expats earning a living in paradise by online day trading. They usually spend a few hours each day researching the financial markets and trading their investments online. Other than market knowledge, which can easily be gained by online research, all you need is an internet connection and an online trading account.

Trading in commodities such as oil, rubber, coffee, gold, silver and uranium is currently popular. There are several ways of benefiting from a commodities bull market, such as buying futures and options, investing in the mining companies, investing in mutual funds which specialize in commodities and even buying the physical commodity.

Some investors purchase metal bars from local gold shops. The gold and silver prices are published daily and local gold shops trade with a margin of approximately $5 per 15.2 grams (Baht Weight) of metal. In Thailand gold jewelry is 96.5% pure, equivalent to 23 karat gold. The alloy is harder than 24 karat pure gold and therefore more durable. Commodities tend to appreciate during times of economic instability. The international gold price (in US$ per ounce) is provided at the **www.kitco.com** website. The market price of gold in Thailand is available online at **www.goldtraders.or.th**.

Futures and Options are financial instruments known as derivatives. A "future" is a binding legal agreement to buy or sell a commodity or other investment. An "option" is a right - but not an obligation - to buy or sell futures

181

contracts during a specified period. Both financial instruments play key roles in helping companies manage risks and lower the cost of doing business.

Some day traders claim massive profits. However others are less successful. Traders should not risk more money than they can afford to lose and obtain financial guidance about the trading risks, systems and procedures. Initially traders are advised to develop their knowledge and experience without investing their money.

SOUTHEAST ASIA DIRECTORY

KEY FACTS FOR SOUTHEAST ASIA

■ ASSOCIATION OF SE ASIAN NATIONS
Internet: www.aseansec.org

■ CLIMATE
Internet: www. climate-charts.com/Locations/
Climate charts for any country in Southeast Asia

■ CURRENCY Exchange Rate Converter
Internet: www.exchange-rates.org/converter.aspx
On 9 February 2010 1US$ =

1.42147	BND	Brunei Dollar
4187.31	KHR	Cambodian Riel
1.000	USD	East Timor, US$
9405.31	IDR	Indonesian Rupiah
8453.88	LAK	Lao Kip
3.44154	MYR	Malaysian Ringgit
6.42933	MMK	Myanmar Kyat
46.585	PHP	Philippine Peso
1.4223	S$	Singapore Dollars
33.1898	THB	Thai Baht
18429.8	VND	Vietnamese Dong

■ EMBASSIES
Internet: www.embassyinformation.com

■ FRANCHISING
Internet: www.franchiselicenseasia.com
www.asiawidefranchise.com (franchise exhibitions)

183

■ HEALTH
Internet: www.cdc.gov/travel/destinations/list.aspx
The Center for Disease Control & Prevention provides comprehensive health advice for each country

■ LAWS
Internet: http://lawasia.asn.au
Asian law directory

■ NEWSPAPERS & MEDIA
Internet: www.abyznewslinks.com
This website lists the media sources for each country

■ PROPERTY
Internet: www. property-report.com
Property Report covers real estate in Asia

■ RADIO STATIONS
Internet: www.asiawaves.net

■ TAXATION
Internet: www.worldwide-tax.com
This website provides guidance on taxation for each country

■ TEACHING JOBS
Internet: www.daveseslcafe.com
Resources and job listings for teachers

■ TIME ZONE CONVERTER
Internet: www.timezoneconverter.com

■ WIFI FINDER
Internet: www.wifinder.com; www.hotspot-locations.com
Searchable databases of wifi zones throughout the world

■ WOMEN
Internet: www.expatwomen.com
Information for expat women

KEY FACTS FOR BRUNEI DARUSSALAM

■ BUSINESS INVESTMENT
Internet: www.bia.com.bn
Email: cla@bia.com.bn
The Brunei Investment Agency

■ CLASSIFIED ADVERTISING
Internet: www.onebrunei.com/classifieds.php
Free classified listings

■ CURRENCY
1US$ = 1.42147 BND (Brunei Dollar) on 9/2/10

■ EMBASSIES
Internet: http://bn.embassyinformation.com/
Locate any embassy for Brunei Darussalam

■ EMPLOYMENT
Internet: www.immigration.gov.bn/working.htm
Issuance of employment visas / passes

■ FLIGHT INFORMATION
Internet: www.brunet.bn
Tel: (673) 233-1747
Database of flight arrivals and departure for Brunei International Airport

■ GOVERNMENT
Internet: www.jpm.gov.bn
Official website of the Prime Minister

■ IMMIGRATION (VISAS)
Internet: www.immigration.gov.bn
Tel: (673) 238-3106
The Immigration Department administers visas

- INFORMATION
Internet: www.tourismbrunei.com
Online information for expats and non residents

- MINISTRY OF EDUCATION
Internet: www.www.moe.edu.bn
Old Airport Road
Berakas BB3510
Tel : +673-2381133
Fax : +673-2380101
Email: feedback@moe.edu.bn

- MINISTRY OF FOREIGN AFFAIRS
Internet: www.mfa.gov.bn
The Ministry of Foreign Affairs & Trade

- NEWSPAPER
Internet: www.bt.com.bn
The Brunei Times is an English-language business newspaper

- POLICE
Internet: www.police.gov.bn
The Royal Brunei Police Force Tel: 993

- RADIO & TELEVISION
Internet: www.rtb.gov.bn

- TIME: GMT + 8 hours

- UNIVERSITI BRUNEI DARUSSALAM
Internet: www.ubd.edu.bn
Tel: (673) 246-3001 Ext:1444
Fax: (673) 246-1003
Email: office.ipro@ubd.edu.bn

- VISAS & WORK PERMITS
Internet: www.immigration.gov.bn/working.htm

KEY FACTS FOR CAMBODIA

■ BUSINESS INVESTMENT
Internet: www.investincambodia.com
Comprehensive information for business investors

■ BUSINESS REGISTRATION
Internet: www.moc.gov.kh
Register your business with the Ministry of Commerce

■ CLASSIFIED ADVERTISING
Internet: www.classifiedscambodia.com
Free classified listings

■ CURRENCY
1US$ = 4187.31 KHR (Cambodian Riel) on 9/2/10

■ CUSTOMS & EXCISE
Internet: www.customs.gov.kh
Guidance on import and export duties

■ EMBASSIES
Internet: http://kh.embassyinformation.com/
Locate any embassy for Cambodia

■ FLIGHT INFORMATION
Internet: www.cambodia-airports.com
Database of flight arrivals and departures

■ GOVERNMENT
Internet: www.cambodia.gov.kh
Official website of the Cambodian government

■ IMMIGRATION (VISAS)
Internet: http://cambodia-immigration.com
Administration of visas

- INFORMATION
Internet: www.cambodia.org; www.canbypublications.com
General information for expats and non residents

- JOBS FOR TEACHERS
Internet: www.daveseslcafe.com

- LAW
Internet: www.cambodia.gov.kh
The legal database is in the Library section

- MAPS
Internet: www.cambodiamaps.blogspot.com

- MINISTRY OF FOREIGN AFFAIRS
Internet: www.mfaic.gov.kh
MFAIC provides consular and travel information

- MINISTRY OF TOURISM
Internet: www.mot.gov.kh
Website provides a business directory

- NEWSPAPERS
Internet: www.cambodiadaily.com;
www.phnompenhpost.com
English-language newspapers

- NGO FORUM
Internet: www.ngoforum.org.kh
Association of NGOs working in Cambodia

- TIME: GMT + 7 hours

■ **TOURIST POLICE**
Internet: www.interior.gov.kh
Tel: 023-726-158
Email: ptd@interior.gov.kh

■ **RADIO**
Internet: http://cambodiaradio.com

ADDITIONAL INFORMATION

■ **BUSINESS**

Cambodia Chamber of Commerce
No. 7D, Confederation de la Russie
Phnom Penh 12156
Tel: (855) 23-880-795
Internet: www.ccc.org.kh
Email: info@ccc.org.kh

Cambodia Special Economic Zone Board
Tel: (855) 23-992-355
Internet: www.cambodiasez.gov.kh
Email: enquiry@cambodiasez.gov.kh

Council for the Development of Cambodia
Government Palace, Sisowath Quay
Wat Phnom, Phnom Penh
Tel: (855) 23-981-154
Fax: (855) 23-428-426
Internet: www.cambodiainvestment.gov.kh
Email: cdc.cib@online.com.kh
Information for business investors

General Department of Customs & Excise
6-8, Norodom Blvd, Phnom Penh
Tel: (855) 23-214-065
Fax: (855) 23-214-065
Internet: www.excise.gov.kh

Ministry of Commerce
Russian Federation Blvd, Toeuk Thla Village,
Sangkat Toeuk Thla, Khan Sen Sok, Phnom Penh
Internet: www.moc.gov.kh

Phnom Penh Chamber of Commerce
Internet: www.ppcc.org.kh

- INFORMATION

Bus Schedules
Internet: http://canbypublications.com/cambodia/buses.htm

Canby Publications
Internet: www.canbypublications.com
This website is a mine of useful information, from bus schedules to travel articles

CIA Factbook on Cambodia
Internet: www.cia.gov/library/publications/the-world-factbook/geos/cb.html

Flight Information
Internet: www.cambodia-airports.com

Ministry of Tourism
Internet: www.mot.gov.kh

■ LAWS & REGULATIONS

Council of Jurists
Internet: www.bigpond.com.kh/Council_of_Jurists/somg.htm
This website provides an indexed database of laws and regulations

■ IMMIGRATION (VISAS)

The Immigration Department of Cambodia
Russian Boulevard (opposite Phnom Penh International Airport)
Tel: (855) 12-581-558
Fax: (855) 23-890-101
Internet: http://cambodia-immigration.com
Email: visa_info@online.com.kh; visa@interior.gov.kh
The Immigration Department administers entry visas for foreigners

Ministry of Foreign Affairs & International Cooperation
Internet: www.mfaic.gov.kh
Email: help@mfaic.gov.kh
The website accepts online tourist visa applications (e-visas)

All nationalities need to apply for a travel visa, except from the following countries: Indonesia, Laos, Malaysia, Myanmar, the Philippines, Singapore, and Vietnam.

A visa on arrival, valid for a thirty-day stay, is specifically granted at Phnom Penh International Airport, Siem Reap International Airport, and International Border Checkpoints. Visas are also granted at Royal Cambodian Embassy or Consulate abroad. The visa fee for a tourist is US$20, and the visa fee for a businessman is US$25. Visas can be extended at Immigration Department in Phnom Penh City. A free visa (K) is expressly granted to the Cambodian living overseas.

The Royal Government of Cambodia has recently approved E-visas. All you have to do is complete the online application form available at the official website (evisa.mfaic.gov.kh), pay by credit card online, and include uploading a recent passport-size photo in JPEG/ PNG format. The visa will be approved within three business days, allowing you to breeze by that lengthy line and get a jumpstart on your holiday.

The E-visa, valid for a thirty-day stay, is available only for a typical tourist visa for a single entry. It is currently not available for nationalities from Iran, Iraq, Pakistan, Afghanistan, Bangladesh, Saudi Arabia, Algeria, Sudan, and Sri Lanka. For a business visa, please apply at your nearest embassy or on arrival in all major check points.

Tourists getting such a visa online can enter Cambodia through Phnom Penh International Airport, Siem Reap International Airport, Bavet (Svay Rieng), Cham Yeam (Koh Kong), and Poipet (Banteay Meanchey), and they can exit through these five main points.

Source: Ministry of Tourism, 10 February 2010

International Checkpoints:

- Phnom Penh International Airport, Kandal
- Angkor International Airport, Siem Reap
- Poi Pet International Border Checkpoint, Banteay Mean Chey

- Cham Yeam International Border Checkpoint, Koh Kong
- Bavet International Border Checkpoint, Svay Rieng
- O'Smach International Border Checkpoint, Odar Mean Chey
- Dong International Border Checkpoint, Battambang
- Prum International Border Checkpoint, Pai Lin
- Phnom Den International Border Checkpoint, Takeo
- Dong Kralor International Border Checkpoint, Stoeng Treng
- Kaam Samnor-Koh Rokar International Border Checkpoint, Kandal
- Chorm International Border Checkpoint, Odar Mean Chey
- Sihanoukville International Port, Kampong Som
- Phnom Penh International Port, Kandal
- Onha Mong International Port, Koh Kong

Source: Immigration Department of Cambodia

- MEDIA

The Foreign Correspondents' Club of Phnom Penh
(FCC Phnom Penh)
363 Sisowath Quay
Phnom Penh, Cambodia
Tel: (855) 23-724-014
Fax: (855) 23-427-758
Internet: www.fcccambodia.com
Email: phnompenh@fcccambodia.com
The FCC is the media hub of Cambodia, offering food and beverages in a relaxing environment

The Phnom Penh Post
888 Building F, 8th Floor
Phnom Penh Center
Corner Sothearos & Sihanouk Blvd
Sangat Tonle Bassac
Khan Chamkarmon, Phnom Penh
Tel: (855) 23-214-311
Fax: (855) 23-214-318
Internet: www.phnompenhpost.com
English-language daily newspaper

- TOURIST POLICE

Tourist Police Department
Ministry of Interior
#275 Norodom Blvd., Phnom Penh
Fax/Phone: (855-23)726158
Internet: www.interior.gov.kh
E-Mail: ptd@interior.gov.kh

- UNIVERSITIES

National University of Management, Phnom Penh
Corner of Monivong Blvd. and street 96 (Christopher Howes Street)
Tel: (855) 23-428-120
Fax: (855) 23-427-105
Internet: www.num.edu.kh
Email: num-highedu@yahoo.com

The Royal University of Phnom Penh
Russian Federation Boulevard,
Toul Kork, Phnom Penh, Cambodia.
Tel: (855) 23-883-640
Fax: (855) 23-880-116
Internet: www.rupp.edu.kh
Email: secrctary@rupp.edu.kh

Royal University of Law and Economics (RULE)
Preah Monivong Boulevard, Sangkat Tonle Bassac,
P.O. Box 842, Phnom Penh
Tel: (855) 12-627-446
Fax: (855) 23-214-953
Internet: www.rule.edu.kh
Email: rector@rule.edu.kh; interelarule@yahoo.com

■ VOLUNTEERING

NGO Forum on Cambodia
#9-11 Street 476, Toul Tompong,
P.O. Box 2295, Phnom Penh 3
Tel: (855) 23-214-429
Fax: (855) 23-994-063
Internet: www.ngoforum.org.kh
Email: info@ngoforum.org.kh
NGO members: www.ngoforum.org.kh/eng/core/sublist-membership.php

KEY FACTS FOR EAST TIMOR (TIMOR LESTE)

- CURRENCY: US Dollar (US$)

- EMBASSIES
Internet: http://tp.embassyinformation.com/

- GOVERNMENT
Internet: www.gov.east-timor.org
Email: info@timor-leste.gov.tl
Official website of the government

- IMMIGRATION (VISAS)
Internet: http://migacao.gov.tl
Email: info@migacao.gov.tl
Tel: (670) 727-7421

- INFORMATION
Internet: www.easttimordirectory.net
Online information for expats and non residents

- LAW
Internet: www.easttimorlegalinformation.org

- MINISTRY OF FINANCE
Internet: www.mof.gov.tl

- MINISTRY OF FOREIGN AFFAIRS & COOPERATION
Internet: www.mfac.gov.tp
Tel: (670) 333 9600
Travel and consular information for foreigners

- NGO'S
Internet: www.etan.org
East Timor Action Network provides a comprehensive list of NGOs working in East Timor

- **TIME:** GMT + 9 hours

- **TIMOR DIVERS NETWORK**
Internet: www.congo-pages.org/timordiversnetwork/home.htm

- **TOURISM OFFICE**
Internet: www.turismotimorleste.com
Email: info@.turismotimorleste.com
Tel: (670) 331-0371

- **UNITED NATIONS IN EAST TIMOR**
Internet: www.tl.undp.org
Tel: (670) 723-0328

KEY FACTS FOR INDONESIA

- **BUSINESS INVESTMENT**
Internet: www.bkpm.go.id
Investment Coordinating Board

- **CURRENCY**
US$1.00 = 9405.31 IDR (Indonesian Rupiah) on 9/2/10

- **DEPARTMENT OF FOREIGN AFFAIRS**
Internet: www.deplu.go.id
Consular and travel information for travelers

- **EMBASSIES**
Internet: http://id.embassyinformation.com/

- **EMPLOYMENT PERMITS**
Refer to: www.expat.or.id

- **EXPAT FORUMS**
Internet: www.livinginindonesiaforum.org

- **GOVERNMENT**
Internet: www.indonesia.go.id
National portal for the Republic of Indonesia

- **IMMIGRATION (VISAS)**
Internet: www.imgrasi.go.id/en/
Tel: (62) 2152-2030

- **INFORMATION**
Internet: www.expat.or.id

- **JOBS FOR TEACHERS**
Internet: www.daveseslcafe.com

SOUTHEAST ASIA DIRECTORY - **INDONESIA**

- **MINISTRY OF INDUSTRY**
Internet: www.deeperin.go.id

- **NEWSPAPER**
Internet: www.thejakartapost.com
The Jakarta Post is an English language newspaper

- **NGO'S**
Internet: www.etan.org
List of NGOs working in Indonesia & East Timor

- **POLICE**
Internet: www.polri.go.id
Email: info@polri.go.id
Tel: (62) 1721-8144

- **TIME: GMT + 7 / 8 / 9 hours**

- **TOURISM**
Internet: www.my-indonesia.info

- **VISA INFO**
Internet: www.expat.or.id/info/docs.html
Visa categories and application guidelines

ADDITIONAL INFORMATION

- CHAMBERS OF COMMERCE

American Chamber of Commerce in Indonesia (AmCham)
World Trade Center, 11th floor
Jl. Jend. Sudirman Kav. 29-31
Jakarta Pusat, 12920
Tel: (62) 21-526-2860
Fax: (62) 21-526-2861
Internet: www.amcham.or.id
Email info@amcham.or.id

Indonesia-Australia Business Council (IABC)
World Trade Center, 11th Floor
Jl. Jend. Sudirman Kav. 29-31
Jakarta 12920
Tel: (62) 21-521-1540
Fax: (62) 21-521-1541
Email secretariat@iabc.or.id

British Chamber of Commerce in Indonesia (BritCham)
Wisma Metropolitan I F/15
Jln. Jend. Sudirman Kav. 29 - 31
Jakarta 12920
Tel: (62) 21-522-9453
Fax: (62) 21-527-9135
Internet: www.britcham.or.id
Email bisnis@britcham.or.id

Indonesia Canada Chamber of Commerce (ICCC)
Sampoerna Strategic Square
South Tower 17th floor
Jl. Jend. Sudirman Kav 45
Tel: (62) 21-2555-2243

Fax: (62) 21-5795-1177
Internet: www.iccc.or.id
Email iccc@cbn.net.id

Danish Business Council
Jl. Kencana Permai V no 15
Pondok Indah, Jakarta Selatan
Tel: (62) 21-750-3204
Internet: www.dba.co.id

Finnish Business Council
Embassy of Finland, Menara Rajawali, 9th floor
Jl Mega Kuningan, Lot 5.1, Kuningan, 12950 Jakarta
Tel:.(62) 21-576-1650
Internet: www.finland.or.id

Indonesian French Chamber of Commerce and Industry
Jalan Wijaya II No. 36
Kebayoran Baru, Jakarta 12160
Tel: (62) 21-739-7161
Fax: (62) 21-739-7168
Internet: www.ifcci.com
Email: contacts@ifcci.com

German Indonesian Chamber of Commerce & Industry
Jl. H. Agus Salim No. 115
Jakarta 10310
Tel: (62) 21-315-4685
Fax: (62) 21-315-5276
Internet: www.ekonid.com
Email info@ekonid.or.id

European Business Chamber of Commerce in Indonesia
World Trade Center, 8th Floor
Jl. Jend. Sudirman Kav. 29-31
Jakarta 12920
Tel: (62) 21-521-1650
Fax: (62) 21-521-1651
Internet: www.eurocham.or.id
Email info@eurocham.or.id

Italian Business Association Indonesia (IBAI)
Wisma BRI II, 15th Floor, Suite 1501
Jl. Jend. Sudirman No. 44-46
Jakarta 10210
Tel: (62) 21-571-3540
Fax: (62) 21)-571-9013

- EMERGENCY SERVICES

24 Hour Ambulance Service in Jakarta
702 Anakida Building, 27, Jakarta 12810
Tel: (62) 2-1830-5848

24 Hours Clinic Assistance Penta Medica
Penta Bali Medica, Jalan Teuku Umar Barat-Marlboro No. 88, Denpasar, Bali 80113,
Tel: (62) 36 1744-6144
Internet: www.pentamedica.com

- IMMIGRATION (VISAS)

Department of Foreign Affairs
Jl. Taman Pejambon
No. 6 Jakarta Pusat 10110
Tel: (62) 21-344-1508
Internet: www.deplu.go.id
Email: dipten@deplu.go.id

Directorate General of Immigration
Jl. Rasuna Said Kav 8-9 Kuningan
Jakarta Selatan, Jakarta
Tel: (62) 21-522-4658
Fax: (62) 21-522-4658
Internet: www.imigrasi.go.id

■ NATIONAL AIRLINE

Garuda Indonesia
Jl.. Medan Merdeka Selatan 13, Jakarta 10110
Tel: 0800-1427832, (62) 1-2351-9999
Internet: www.garuda-indonesia.com

KEY FACTS FOR LAOS (LAO P. D. R.)

- BUSINESS INVESTMENT
Internet: www.invest.laopdr.org; www.laotrade.org.la

- BUSINESS REGISTRATION
Internet: www.moic.gov.la

- CLASSIFIED ADVERTISING
Internet: www.findinlaos.com
Free classified listings

- CURRENCY
US$1.00 = 8453.88 LAK (Lao Kip) on 9/2/10

- EMBASSIES
Internet: http://la.embassyinformation.com/

- FLIGHT INFORMATION
Internet: www.laoairlines.com

- GOVERNMENT
Internet: www.laopdr.gov.la

- IMMIGRATION (VISAS)
Internet: www.mofa.gov.la

- INFORMATION
Internet: www.laos-travel.com

- JOBS
Internet: http://lao-advertising.com
Database of jobs

- LAW
Internet: www.na.gov.la
The National Assembly lists the laws of Laos

- **MINISTRY OF FOREIGN AFFAIRS (MOFA)**
Internet: www.mofa.gov.la
Consular and travel information for foreigners

- **NATIONAL UNIVERSITY OF LAOS**
Internet: www.nuol.edu.la
Email: nuol@nuol.edu.la
Tel: (856) 2177-0068

- **NEWSPAPER**
Internet: www.vientianetimes.org.la
The Vientiane Times is an English language newspaper

- **NGO'S**
Internet: www.directoryofngos.org
List of NGOs working in Laos

- **TIME: GMT + 7 hours**

- **TOURISM**
Internet: www.tourismlaos.org
Tel: (856) 2121-2248
Lao National Tourism Administration

- **UNITED NATIONS DEVELOPMENT PROGRAMME (UNDP) IN LAOS**
Internet: www.undplao.org
Also refer to: www.unlao.org

- **VIENTIANE COLLEGE**
Internet: www.vientianecollege.com
Email: info@vientianecollege.com
Tel: (856) 2141-4873

ADDITIONAL INFORMATION

■ BUSINESS

Ministry of Industry and Commerce
Phon Xay Rd, P.O.Box 4107 Vientiane
Tel: (856) 2191-1342
Fax: (856) 2141-2434
Email: citd@moic.gov.la

■ IMMIGRATION

Ministry of Foreign Affairs
01004, 23 Singha Road, Vientiane
Tel: (856) 2141-3148
Fax: (856) 2141-4009
Internet: www.mofa.gov.la
Email: ict@mofa.gov.la

■ INTERNATIONAL CHECK-POINTS

1. Houayxay (Lao) - Xiengkhong (Thai)
2. Thakhek (Lao) - Nakhonphanom (Thai)
3. Savannakhet (Lao) - Mukdahan (Thai)
4. Vangtao (Lao) - Xongmek (Thai)
5. Namphao (Lao) - Cautreo (Vietnam)
6. Densavanh (Lao) - Laobao (Vietnam)
7. Naphao (Lao) - Chalo (Vietnam)
8. Boten (Lao) - Bohane (China)
9. Namkane (Lao) - Namekane (Vietnam)
10. Namsoue (Lao) - Nameo (Vietnam)
11. Parksane (Lao) - Beungkane (Thai)
12. Wattay International Airport.
13. Louang Prabang International Airport.
14. Friendship Bridge

INTERNATIONAL ORGANIZATIONS IN LAOS

Asian Development Bank
Lao Resident Office, The Novotel Hotel,
Luang Prabang Road, P.O.Box 9724, Vientiane
Tel: (856) 2121 -9098
Fax: (856) 2121-9096.

Food and Agriculture Organization
Phonxay Road, Vientiane
Tel: (856) 2141 4503
Fax: (856) 2141 4500.

International Monetary Fund
Bank of the Lao PDR, Vientiane
Tel: (856) 2121-3106
Fax: (856) 2121-4986.

United Nations Development Programme
Phonkheng Road, P.O.Box 345, Vientiane
Tel: (856) 2121-3390
Fax: (856) 2121-4819

United Nations Population Fund
Ban Phonxay, Phonxay Road, P.O. Box 345, Vientiane
Tel: (856) 2141-3467
Fax: (856) 2141-2398.

United Nations High Commission for Regugees
Phonkheng Road, Vientiane
Tel: (856) 2121-2038
Fax: (856) 2121-3385.

United Nations Children's Fund
Wat Nak Quarter, Km 3, Thadeua Road,
P.O.Box 1080, Vientiane
Tel: (856) 2131-5200
Fax: (856) 2131-4 852.

United Nations International Drug Control Programme
Phonkheng Road, Vientiane
Tel: (856) 2141-3204

International Red Cross
Setthathirath Road (Soi Xieng Nhune), Vientiane
Tel: (856) 2121-5762
Fax: (856) 2121-5935.

World Bank
Ban Phonxay, Nehru Road, P.O.Box 345, Vientiane
Tel: (856) 2141-4209
Fax: (856) 2141-4210

World Food Programme
Phonkheng Road, P.O.Box 345, Vientiane
Tel: (856) 2121-3390

World Health Organization
Phonxay Quarter, Vientiane
Tel:(856) 2141-3431
Fax: (856) 2141-3432.

Source: Lao National Tourism Administration

■ VISA CATEGORIES

Diplomatic visas (A1)

Diplomatic visas are issued to diplomats, consular officers, heads of the United Nations Agencies and other International Organizations, and their dependents (spouse and children) holding diplomatic passports.

Diplomatic visas (A1) and official visas (A2) are exempted from visa fees. Multiple entry visas may be obtained for a period of one year and may be renewed each year until the assignment's completion.

Official visas (A2)

Official visas are issued to the Staff members of Diplomatic Missions, Consulates, United Nations Agencies and other International Agencies and their dependents (spouse and children) holding official passports.

Courtesy visas (B1)

Courtesy visas are issued to foreign experts and their dependents holding diplomatic, official and ordinary passports performing assignments under bilateral cooperation or grant assistance projects for the Government of Lao PDR.

Courtesy visas (B1) are exempted from visa fees. Multiple entry visas may be obtained for a period of six months and may be renewed every six months until the assignment's completion.

Business Visas (B2)

Business visas are issued to foreign experts performing assignments under projects provided by loan agreements and as provided by employment contracts or project wards, to experts and volunteers of Non-Governmental Agencies, experts in education and medical sciences generating income for an agency, staff members of Diplomatic Missions, General Consulates, the United Nations Agencies and other international organizations holding ordinary passports from the countries or from third countries, as well as foreign businesspersons.

Business visas (B2) are subject to the payment of mandatory visa and service fees. Multiple entry visas may be obtained for a period of one (1) year, six (6) months and three (3) months and may be renewed every one (1) year, six- (6) months and three (3) months until completion of assignments.

Visit visas (B3)

Visit visas are issued to foreign citizens holding ordinary passports and intending to visit relatives working in the Lao PDR.

Visit visa (B3) are subject to the payment of visa and service fees upon each travel in destination to the Lao PDR. B3 visas do not entitle its holder to work or apply for multiple entry visas.

Tourist Visas: (T)

Tourist Visas are issued to foreign visitors for their excursion and enjoy sightseeing in Lao the tourist visas valid for 15 days entering and staying permit in the territory of the Lao PDR. Embassies or General Consulates of the Lao PDR gives those tourist visas. Overseas or Lao authorities at the International Check Points which have had full right obtain tourist visas upon arrival in accordance with their stem employment prohibited.

Transit Visas: (TR)

Transit visas are issued to foreign visitors who transit through the Lao PDR. to third country including their air tickets the Embassies or General Consulates of the Lao PDR. at abroad has had full right obtain transit visas with its two voyages and stem These "Employment prohibited" visas are allowed to stay permit in the Lao PDR.for the period 7 days only

Source: Ministry of Foreign Affairs, 19 February 2010

KEY FACTS FOR MALAYSIA

- BUSINESS INVESTMENT
Internet: www.mida.gov.my

- BUSINESS REGISTRATION
Internet: www.ssm.com.my

- CLASSIFIED ADVERTISING
Internet: www.expatkl.com; www.business.com.my
Free classified listings

- CURRENCY
US$1.00 = 3.44154 MYR (Malaysian Ringgit) on 9/2/10

- EMBASSIES
Internet: http://my.embassyinformation.com/

- EMPLOYMENT
Internet: www.mohr.gov.my
The Ministry of Human Resources administers employment passes

- ENVIRONMENTAL NGO'S
Internet: www.mengo.org
Malaysia Environmental NGOs

- FLIGHT INFORMATION
Internet: www.klia.com.my
KLIA Tel: (603) 8776-2000
http://lcct.klia.com.my
Database of flight arrivals and departures

- GOVERNMENT
Internet: www.parliamen.gov.my; www.malaysia.gov.my

■ IMMIGRATION (VISAS)
Internet: www.imi.gov.my
Tel: (603) 2095-5077

■ INFORMATION
Internet: www.expatkl.com
Email: helpdesk@mm2h.com
General information and forums for expats

■ JOBS DIRECTORY
Internet: www.malaysiajobs.org
Links to recruitment agencies and databases

■ LAW
Internet: www.lawnet.com.my
Malaysian law directory

■ MALAYSIA SECOND HOME PROGRAMME
Internet: www.mm2h.com; www.mm2h.gov.my
Government incentives to attract foreign investment including 10 year visa

■ MINISTRY OF FOREIGN AFFAIRS
Internet: www.kln.gov.my
Consular and travel information for foreigners

■ PROPERTY
Internet: www.propertyinmalaysia.com

■ RAILWAY
Internet: www.ktmb.com.my
Railway connecting Singapore with Thailand

■ RETIREMENT IN MALAYSIA
Refer to the Malaysia Second Home Programme:
www.mm2h.gov.my

- TIME: GMT + 8 hours

- TOURISM MALAYSIA
Internet: www.tourism.gov.my
Tel: (603) 2615-8188

- TOURIST POLICE
Internet: www.idc-pro-malaysia.com
Tel: (603) 2149-6590

- VOLUNTEERING
Internet: www.thaingo.org
This website offers job listings of Thai NGOs

- WORKING
Internet: www.imi.gov.my
The Immigration Department issues employment passes

ADDITIONAL INFORMATION

- BUSINESS

Companies Commission of Malaysia
Tingkat 2 & 10-19, Putra Place,
100 Jalan Putra,
50622 Kuala Lumpur.
Tel : (603) 4047-6000
Fax : (603) 4047-6111 / 6222
Internet: www.ssm.com.my
Email: enquiry@ssm.com.my
Company registration in Malaysia

■ EMPLOYMENT

Kementerian Sumber Manusia (Ministry of Human Resources)
Government of Malaysia
Level 2-4, Block B (North), Jalan Damanlela, Pusat Bandar Damansara,
50530 Kuala Lumpur
Tel: (603) 3255-7200
Fax: (603) 3255-4700
Internet: www.mohr.gov.my
Email: mhr@po.jaring.my
Administration of Employment Passes in Malaysia

■ MALAYSIA MY SECOND HOME PROGRAMME (MM2H)

The MM2H programme is open to qualified foreign individuals who want a second home in Malaysia, and who intend to retire there. For further details, refer to the website, www.mm2h.com.

Eligibility

The programme is open to all foreign citizens from countries recognised by Malaysia. The exclusion of foreign spouses of Malaysian citizens was removed in February 2009 and they are now allowed to apply for the MM2H visa.

Effective 2009 applicants are not required to use the services of an approved government agent. If you do choose to use an agent they must be authorised by the Ministry of Tourism. These companies have the initials "MM2H" in the company name.

Borneo Vision (MM2H) Sdn Bhd is an approved agent for the programme. If you use an agent the initial application can be made without even coming to Malaysia. You will only have to be in Malaysia when the letter of "conditional approval" is issued and you complete the remaining conditions and collect the visa. If you use an agent there is no need for a police report as the agent will sponsor you.

Upon Application – Financial Criteria

Applicants are required to show they have sufficient financial resources to live in Malaysia without seeking employment or other assistance from the government.

Applicants under 50 are required to show liquid assets above RM500,000 and a monthly income of over RM10,000 (equivalent).

Applicants over 50 have show assets over RM350,000 and monthly income of RM10,000. Applicants receiving a government pension over RM10,000 a month will be exempted from making the Fixed Deposit.

Acceptable assets for people over 50 include cash in the bank, bonds, securities and property.

Upon Approval – Fixed Deposit

Approved applicants over 50 receiving a pension from a government in excess of RM10,000 can request exemption from making any Fixed Deposit

i) Applicants aged below 50 years old:

- Must place a Fixed Deposit in a bank account in Malaysia of RM300,000.

- Can withdraw up to RM150,000 for the purchase of house, medical insurance or children's education expenses after the deposit has been placed for one year

- Must maintain a minimum balance of RM150,000 from second year onwards and throughout stay in Malaysia under this programme.

ii) Applicants aged 50 years and above:

- Must place a Fixed Deposit in a bank account in Malaysia of RM150,000

- Can withdraw up to RM50,000 of the fixed deposit after one year to purchase of house, medical insurance or children's education expenses.

- Must maintain a minimum balance of RM100,000 throughout their stay in Malaysia under this programme.

iii) Applicants who have purchased a house (or houses) with a total value of RM1 million and above.

- Must show evidence of ownership and payments amounting to a minimum of RM150,000 if over 50 and RM300,000 if under 50 (i.e. the amount they would have otherwise had to place on fixed deposit)

- Must have been purchased within 5 years of application for MM2H visa

- Will have to place a Fixed Deposit in a bank account in Malaysia of RM150,000 if under 50 and RM100,000 if over 50.

It should be noted that the fixed deposit does not have to be placed until after the applicant has received a letter of "conditional approval". This letter sets out the steps that have to be completed before the visa is issued. This usually consists of placing the Fixed Deposit, having a medical examination in Malaysia and obtaining medical insurance for Malaysia. Once these steps are completed the visa can be collected from the Immigration Department in Putrajaya.

Employment/Business Investment

In February 2009 the government announced that MM2H visa holders 50 years old and above could work for up to 20 hours a week. This is applicable to visa holders who have specialised skills in certain approved sectors. We are advised the decision on whether to approve part time work is based on the approving committee view on whether a Malaysian could do the job.

It was also announced that MM2Hers will also be permitted to set up, and invest in businesses in Malaysia. They will be subject to the same regulations as other foreign investors but will be permitted to actively participate in the running for the business.

Sponsor/Assistance

All applicants require a sponsor and the agent is required to do this. This service is included in their standard fee.

Insurance Coverage / Medical Report

Applicants and their dependants must possess a medical insurance coverage from any insurance company that is valid in Malaysia. This may be waived for older applicants who are denied coverage because of their age. All applicants and their dependants are required to have a medical examination from any private hospital or registered clinic in Malaysia. Both these conditions are met after the letter of "conditional approval" is issued.

Dependents

Applicants are allowed to bring along their dependants (children below 21 years of age, step children, disabled children, and parents) under their MM2H visa. Older dependent children will have to get a separate visa.

Dependants attending school in Malaysia are also required to apply for a Student Pass which allows them to continue their education in schools or Institutions of Higher Learning recognised by the government.

House Purchase

Each participant is allowed to purchase an unlimited number of residences at a minimum of 250,000 per unit. All purchases must be approved by the state authorities and certain types of properties cannot be purchased e,g those on 'Malay Reserve' land

Parents and Taxes

Successful applicants are bound by the policies, systems and regulations of taxes of this country however their overseas income will not be taxed in Malaysia.

Security Vetting

Approvals are given subject to security vetting clearance conducted by the Royal Malaysian Police.

Restrictions

Successful applicants are not permitted to participate in activities that can be considered as sensitive to the local people like political or missionary activities.

Source: www.mm2h.com

■ TOURIST INFORMATION

Tourism Malaysia HQ
17th Floor, Menara Dato' Onn, Putra World Trade Centre,
45, Jalan Tun Ismail,
50480 Kuala Lumpur
Tel: (603) 2615-8188
Fax: (603) 2693-5884
Tourism Infoline: 1-300-88-5050 (within Malaysia only)
Email: enquiries@tourism.gov.my

■ RADIO & TV

Radio & TV Stations
Internet: www.mycen.com.my/malaysia/radio_tv.html

KEY FACTS FOR MYANMAR

- BORDER CROSSINGS
Tachileik (Mae Sai), Myawadi* (Mae Sot), Kawthoung, Payathonzu* (* indicates daytime entry only)

- BUSINESS INVESTMENT
Internet: www.dica.gov.mm/investmentguide.htm

- BUSINESS REGISTRATION
Internet: www.commerce.gov.mm

- CURRENCY
US$1.00 = 6.42933 MMK (Myanmar Kyat) on 9/2/10

- EMBASSIES
Internet: http://mm.embassyinformation.com/

- GOVERNMENT
Internet: www.myanmar.gov.mm

- INFORMATION
Internet: www.myanmar.com;
www.myanmartravelinformation.com

- MAGAZINE
Internet: www.irrawaddy.org
International magazine for Myanmar

- MINISTRY OF FOREIGN AFFAIRS (MOFA)
Internet: www.mofa.gv.mm
Consular and travel information for foreigners

- MINISTRY OF INDUSTRY
Internet: www.industry1myanmar.com

- **MINISTRY OF TRANSPORT**
Internet: www.mot.gov.mm
Tel: +95-67-411039

- **NEWSPAPER**
Internet: www.myanmartimes.com.mm
The Myanmar Times is an English language newspaper

- **NGO'S**
Internet: www.ngoinmyanmar.org
NGO forums, jobs and directory for Myanmar

- **POLICE**
Internet: www.myanmar.gov.mm/ministry/home/MPFmain.htm

- **TIME: GMT + 6 ½ hours**

- **TOURISM**
Internet: www.hotels-tourism.gov.mm
The Ministry of Hotels and Tourism

- **WORK PERMITS**
Internet: www.myanmarvisa.com
Private visa consultancy

KEY FACTS FOR THE PHILIPPINES

■ BUSINESS INVESTMENT
Internet: www.boi.gov.ph
The Board of Investment provides incentives for foreign investors

■ BUSINESS REGISTRATION
Internet: http://.business.gov.ph
Register your business with the Philippine Business Registry

■ CLASSIFIED ADVERTISING
Internet: www.olx.com.ph
Free classified listings

■ CURRENCY
1US$ = 46.585 PHP (Philippine Peso) on 9/2/10

■ DEPARTMENT OF FOREIGN AFFAIRS (DFA)
Internet: http://dfa.gov.ph
Travel and consular guidance for foreigners

■ DEPARTMENT OF TOURISM
Internet: www.tourism.gov.ph
Tel: (632) 523-8411

■ DEPARTMENT OF TRADE & INDUSTRY
Internet: www.dti.gov.ph
Tel: (632) 751-3330

■ EMBASSIES
Internet: http://ph.embassyinformation.com/

■ FLIGHT INFORMATION
Internet: www.manila-airport.net
Database of flight arrivals and departures

- **GOVERNMENT**
Internet: www.gov.ph
Official website of the Philippine government

- **IMMIGRATION (VISAS)**
Internet: www.immigration.gov.ph

- **INFORMATION**
Internet: www.myph.com.ph; www.livinginthephilippines.com
Online forums for expats and non residents

- **LAW**
Internet: www.lawphil.net/statutes/statutes.html
Index of Philippine laws & regulations

- **MAPS**
Internet: www.philsite.net
Travel website

- **NEWSPAPER**
Internet: www.mb.com.ph
The Manila Bulletin is an English-language newspaper

- **NGO'S**
Internet: www.pcnc.com.ph
Accreditation and register of NGOs

- **POLICE**
Internet: www.pnp.gov.ph/
Tel: (632) 723-0401 (24 hours)

- **RADIO**
Internet: www.thefilipino.com/radio

- **RECRUITMENT**
Internet: www.bestjobs.com.ph
Recruitment database

- **TAXATION & WORK PERMITS**
Internet: www.bir.gov.ph
The Bureau of Internal Revenue administers taxation

- **TIME: GMT + 8 hours**

ADDITIONAL INFORMATION

- **BUSINESS**

Association of Filipino Franchisers, Inc. (AFFI)
Unit 3A, Classica I Condominium, 112 H.V. dela Costa St., Makati City
Tel: (632) 813-5836
Fax: (632) 819-0007
Internet: www.filfranchisers.com
Email: info@filfranchisers.com

Board of Investments (BOI)
Industry and Investments Bldg.,
385 Sen. Gil Puyat Ave., Makati City, Manila
Tel: (632) 897-6682
Internet: www.boi.gov.ph

Business Guide
Internet: www.philippinebusiness.com.ph/guide/prc01.htm

Cagayan Economic Zone Authority
7th Floor Westar Building, 611 Shaw Blvd., Pasig City
Internet: www.cagayanfreeport.com

Clark Development Corporation
Building 2122, E. Quirino Ave., Clark Special Economic Zone, Clark Field, Pampanga
Tel: (045) 589-2092
Internet: www.clark.com.ph

John Hay Poro Point Development Corporation
Loakan Road, Baguio City
Tel: (074) 442-7902

Ministry of Foreign Affairs & Trade
Internet: www.mfa.gov.bn

Philippine Chamber of Commerce & Industry (PCCI)
14/F Multinational Bancorp Center, 6805 Ayala Ave., Makati City
Tel: (632) 843-3374
Fax: (632) 843-4102
Internet: www.philcham.com
Email: pcciindr@mozcom.com

Philippine Business Registry
Internet: http://business.gov.ph
Email: pbr-pmu@dti.gov.ph

Philippine Economic Zone Authority (PEZA)
Roxas Boulevard, Cor. San Luis St., Pasay City
Tel: (632) 551-3454
Internet: www.peza.gov.ph

Philippine Information Agency
PIA Building, Visayas Avenue, Diliman, Quezon City 1101
Internet: www.pia.gov.ph

Philippine Marketing Association, Inc. (PMA)
Suite 2414, Cityland 10, Tower 1, 6815 Ayala Ave.,
Cor. H.V. dela Costa St., Makati City
Tel: (632) 893-7127
Email: pma@philonline.com.ph

Subic Bay Metropolitan Authority (SBMA)
Building 229, Waterfront Road, Subic Bay Freeport,
Olongapo City
Tel. (63-47) 252-4242
Internet: www.sbma.com

Zamboanga Economic Zone Authority
San Ramon, Zamboanga City
Tel: (062) 992-2012
Internet: www.zambofreeport.com

DOING BUSINESS IN THE PHILIPPINES

Workforce

The Filipino workforce is one of the most compelling advantages the Philippines has over any other Asian country. With higher education priority, the literacy rate in the country is 94.6% -- among the highest. English is taught in all schools, making the Philippines the world's third largest English-speaking country. Every year, there are some 350,000 graduates enriching the professional pool.

Strategic business location

The Philippines is located right in the heart of Asia – today the fastest growing region. It is located within four hours flying time from major capitals of the region. Sited at the crossroads of the eastern and western business, it is a critical entry point to over 500 million people in the Association of Southeast Asian Nations (ASEAN) market and a gateway of international shipping and air lanes suited for European and American businesses.

First-class lifestyle

Discover the best of sun, sea, sand and style in the tropical setting teeming with the best of western amenities. The Philippines is second home to expatriates who enjoy the company of the warmest people in the region, the country's openness to varied cultures, and a decidedly global outlook. Expats enjoy accessible and affordable luxuries – business centers, housing, schools, hospitals, shopping malls, hotels and restaurants, beach resorts, and recreation centers.

Abundant resources

An archipelago like the Philippines offers diverse natural resources, from land to marine to mineral resources. It is also the biggest copper producer in Southeast Asia and among the top ten producers of gold in the world. It is also home to 2,145 fish species, four times more than those found in the Bahamas. The 7,100 islands boast of beautiful beaches and breathtaking sceneries that offer soothing leisure and relaxation spots for vacationers and tourists.

Low cost of doing business

Wages are typically less than a fifth of that in the United States. Local communication, electricity, and housing costs are also 50% lower compared to the US rates. Foreign companies that are now outsourcing programming and business processes to the Philippines estimate 30%-40% business cost savings, 15%-30% call center services and application systems, and 35%-50% software development.

Liberalized and business-friendly economy

An open economy, like the Philippines, allows 100% foreign ownership in almost all sectors and supports a Build-Operate-Transfer (BOT) investment scheme that other Asian countries emulate. Government corporations are being privatized and the banking, insurance, shipping telecommunications, and power industries have been deregulated. Incentive packages include the corporate income tax, reduced to a current 32%, with companies in the Special Economic Zones (ecozones) subject to only 5% overall tax rates. Multinationals looking for regional headquarters are entitled to incentives such as tax exemptions and tax and duty-free importation of specific equipment and materials.

Unlimited business opportunities

As Asian economies integrate within the vast framework of the ASEAN Free Trade Agreement (AFTA), the Philippines is the natural and most strategic location for firms that want access to the large ASEAN market and its vast trade opportunities. The Philippines has enhanced and primed up various areas for investors and offers a dynamic consumer market accustomed to an array of product choices created by a competitive domestic economy.

Developing Infrastructure for global growth

A well-developed communication, transportation, business, and economic infrastructure links the three major islands -- Luzon, Visayas, and Mindanao -- and distinguishes the Philippine economy. Highly accessible by air, water, and cyberspace, liberalization of inter-island shipping and domestic aviation further sparked improved facilities and services. The container terminals are suited to handle cargo traffic at the highest levels of efficiency.

Communication provides redundant international connectivity 24/7 with fiber optic cable as primary backbone network and satellite as backup. Economic reforms emphasize regional growth, converting remote areas into business centers.

The landmark BOT legislation allows private investors to build and operate infrastructure, then turn it over to the Philippine government after a set period of time.

The Philippines offer state-of-the-art telecommunications facilities, adequate and uninterrupted power supply. There are ready-to-occupy offices and production facilities, computer security and building monitoring systems, as well as complete office services in specialized information technology (IT) zones. With the government's focus on building up an IT-enabled economy, the Philippines is on its way to becoming the E-services Hub of Asia.

Source: Philippine Business Registry, 11 February 2010

■ EDUCATION

Commission on Higher Education
Internet: www.ched.gov.ph

Department of Education
Internet: www.deped.gov.ph
The website allows free download of lists of public and private schools

Southeast Asian Ministers of Education Organization
Internet: www.seameo.org

Technical Education and Skills Development Authority
Internet: www.tesda.gov.ph

■ EMPLOYMENT

Department of Labor & Employment (DOLE)
Muralla St., Corner Gen. Luna St.,
Intramuros, 1002 Manila
Tel: (632) 908-2917
Internet: www.dole.gov.ph

■ IMMIGRATION

Bureau of Immigration
2nd Floor Bureau of Immigration Bldg.
Magallanes Drive, Intramuros, Manila
Tel: (632) 527-3248
Fax: (632) 309-7751
Internet: http://immigration.gov.ph/index.php
Email: mclibanan@immigration.gov.ph

Department of Foreign Affairs (DFA)
2330 Roxas Boulevard
Pasay City
Tel: (632) 834-4000
Internet: http://dfa.gov.ph
The DFA administers visa applications

GUIDELINES ON THE ENTRY OF TEMPORARY VISITOR TO THE PHILIPPINES

Nationals from countries listed below who are traveling to the Philippines for business and tourism purposes are allowed to enter the Philippines without visas for a stay not exceeding twenty-one (21) days, provided they hold valid tickets for their return journey to port of origin or next port of destination and their passports valid for a period of at least six (6) months beyond the contemplated period of stay. However, Immigration Officers at ports of entry may exercise their discretion to admit holders of passports valid for at least sixty (60) days beyond the intended period of stay.

Nationals from the following countries are allowed to enter the Philippines without a visa for a period of stay of twenty-one (21) days or less:

Andorra; Angola; Antigua and Barbuda; Argentina; Australia Austria; Bahamas; Bahrain; Barbados; Belgium; Benin; Bhutan; Bolivia; Botswana; Brazil*; Brunei; Bulgaria; Burkina Faso; Burundi; Cambodia; Cameroon; Canada; Cape Verde; Central African Republic; Chad; Chile; Colombia; Comoros; Congo; Costa Rica; Cote d'Ivoire; Cyprus; Czech Republic; Democratic Republic of the

SOUTHEAST ASIA DIRECTORY - **PHILIPPINES**

Congo; Denmark; Djibouti; Dominica; Dominican Republic; Ecuador; El Salvador; Equatorial Guinea; Eritrea; Estonia; Ethiopia; Fiji; Finland; France; Gabon; Gambia; Germany; Ghana; Gibraltar; Greece; Grenada; Guatemala; Guinea; Guinea Bissau; Guyana; Haiti; Honduras; Hungary; Iceland; Indonesia; Ireland; Israel*; Italy; Jamaica; Japan; Kenya; Kiribati; Kuwait; Lao People's Democratic Republic; Latvia; Lesotho; Liberia; Liechtenstein; Lithuania; Luxembourg; Madagascar; Malawi; Malaysia; Maldives; Mali; Malta; Marshall Islands; Mauritania; Mauritius; Mexico; Micronesia; Monaco; Mongolia; Morocco; Mozambique; Myanmar; Namibia; Nepal; Netherlands; New Zealand; Nicaragua; Niger; Norway; Oman; Palau; Panama; Papua New Guinea; Paraguay; Peru; Poland; Portugal; Qatar; Republic of Korea; Romania; Russia; Rwanda; Saint Kitts and Nevis; Saint Lucia; Saint Vincent and the Grenadines; Samoa; San Marino; Sao Tome and Principe; Saudi Arabia; Senegal; Seychelles; Singapore; Slovakia; Slovenia; Solomon Islands; Somalia; South Africa; Spain; Suriname; Swaziland; Sweden; Switzerland; Thailand; Togo; Trinidad and Tobago; Tunisia; Turkey; Tuvalu; Uganda; United Arab Emirates; United Kingdom of Great Britain and Northern Ireland; United Republic of Tanzania; United States of America; Uruguay; Venezuela; Vietnam; Zambia; Zimbabwe.

* The following are allowed to enter the Philippines without a visa for a stay not exceeding fifty-nine (59) days:

- Holders of Brazil passports; and
- Holders of Israel passports

233

The following are allowed to enter the Philippines without a visa for a stay not exceeding seven (7) days:

- Holders of Hong Kong Special Administrative (SAR) passports
- Holders of British National Overseas (BNO) passports
- Holders of Portuguese Passports issued in Macao
- Holders of Macao Special Administrative Region (SAR) passports

Important Note:

Nationals who are subjects of deportation/blacklist orders of the Department and the Bureau of Immigration shall not be admitted to the Philippines. Further inquiries may be addressed to the Visa Division (Telephone numbers: 834-4854, 834-3707, and 834-4810), Department of Foreign Affairs, 2330 Roxas Boulevard, Pasay City or to any Philippine Embassy or Consulate abroad.

Source: Department of Foreign Affairs, 11 February 2010

- MEDIA

The Manila Bulletin
Muralla corner Recoletos
Intramuros, Manila 1002
P.O. BOX 769
Tel: (632) 527-8121
Fax: (632) 527-7510
Internet: www.mb.com.ph
Email: bulletin@mb.com.ph

NGO'S

Philippine Council for NGO Certification (PCNC)
6th Floor SCC Bldg., CFA-MA Compound 4427 Interior
Old Sta. Mesa 1016 Manila
Tel: (632) 782-15-68
Fax: (632) 715-27-83
Internet: www.pcnc.com.ph
E-mail: pcnc@pldtdsl.net
Certification and register of NGOs in the Philippines

POLICE

Philippine National Police
Tel: (632) 723-0401 (24 hours)
Internet: www.pnp.gov.ph/
Email: feedback@pnp.gov.ph

TRAVEL & TOURISM

Department of Tourism
T.F. Valencia Circle
T.M. Kalaw St., Rizal Park, Manila
Tel: (632) 523-8411
Internet: www.tourism.gov.ph
Email: webmaster@tourism.gov.ph

TAXATION

Bureau of Internal Revenue (BIR)
BIR National Office Bldg.,
Agham Road, Diliman, Quezon City
Tel: (632) 929-7676
Internet: www.bir.gov.ph
Email: contact_us@cctr.bir.gov.ph
BIR is responsible for taxation and work permits

KEY FACTS FOR SINGAPORE

- BUSINESS
Internet: www.mof.gov.sg
The Ministry of Finance regulates business in Singapore

- EDUCATION
Internet: www.moe.edu.sg

- EMBASSIES
Internet: http://sg.embassyinformation.com/

- EMPLOYMENT
Internet: www.mom.gov.sg
The Ministry of Manpower provides comprehensive information about working in Singapore

- HEALTH
Internet: www.moh.gov.sg

- IMMIGRATION (VISAS)
Internet: www.ica.gov.sg www.entersingapore.info
The Immigration & Checkpoints Authority

- INFORMATION
Internet: www.ecitizen.gov.sg; www.singaporeexpats.com
General information for expats and non residents

- JOBS
Internet: http://contactsingapore.jobscentral.com.sg

- MINISTRY OF FOREIGN AFFAIRS
Internet: www.mfa.gov.sg
Consular and travel information for foreigners

SOUTHEAST ASIA DIRECTORY - **SINGAPORE**

■ LAW
Internet: http://statutes.agc.gov.sg
Online database of Singaporean statutes

■ LICENSES & PERMITS
Internet: www.business.gov.sg
Enterprise One is an agency of the Singapore government

■ POLICE
Internet: www.spf.gov.sg
Tel: (65) 6353-0000

■ THE STRAITS TIMES
Internet: www.straitstimes.com
The primary English language newspaper of Singapore

■ TIME: GMT + 8 hours

■ TRANSPORT & TRAVEL
Internet: http://tt.ecitizen.gov.sg/index.htm

Bus Information: www.sbstransit.com.sg

Changi Airport: www.changiairport.com

Land Transport Authority: www.lta.gov.sg

Train & Bus Schedules: www.smrt.com.sg

ADDITIONAL INFORMATION

- BUSINESS

Enterprise One
Internet: www.business.gov.sg
Enterprise One is a governmental agency which offers a gateway to business resources in Singapore and provides information on business permits and licensing

Ministry of Finance
#10-01 and #06-03 The Treasury
100 High Street Singapore 179434
Tel: (65) 622-9911
Fax: (65) 6332-7435
Internet: www.mof.gov.sg
Email: mof_qsm@mof.gov.sg

Ministry of Trade And Industry (MTI)
100 High Street, #09-01 The Treasury, Singapore 179434
Tel: (65) 6225-9911
Fax: (65) 6332-7260
Internet: www.mti.gov.sg
Email: mti_email@mti.gov.sg
The purpose of MTI is to promote economic growth and create jobs so as to achieve higher standards of living for all

- CONTACTS FOR TEACHERS

British Council
30 Napier Road
Singapore 258509
Tel: (65) 6473-1111
Fax: (65) 6472-1010
Internet: www.britishcouncil.org
Email: via website form

International Schools
Internet: www.entersingapore.info/sginfo/education.php

Ministry of Education
1 North Buona Vista Drive, Singapore, 138675
Tel: (65) 6872-2220
Fax: (65) 6775-5826
Internet: www.moe.edu.sg
Email: contact@moe.edu.sg

Schools in Singapore
Internet: www3.moe.edu.sg/schdiv/sis/

■ HEALTH

Ministry of Health
College of Medicine Building 16
College Road, Singapore 169854
Tel: (65) 6325-9220
Fax: (65) 6224-1677
Internet: www.moh.gov.sg
Email: moh_info@moh.gov.sg

■ INFORMATION

Ministry of Information, Communications And The Arts
140 Hill Street #02-02 MICA Building Singapore 179369
Tel: (65) 6270-7988
Fax: (65) 6837-9480
Internet: www.mica.gov.sg
Email: mica@mica.gov.sg
The purpose of MICA is to develop Singapore as a global city for information, Communications and the arts, so as to build a creative economy, gracious community and a connected society with a Singaporean identity rooted in our multicultural heritage

■ POLICE

Singapore Police Headquarters
New Phoenix Park
28 Irrawaddy Road
Singapore 329560
Tel: (65) 6353-0000
Internet: www.spf.gov.sg

■ SOCIAL CLUBS

Alliance Francaise
1, Sarkies Road
Tel: (65) 6737-8422

American Association of Singapore
21 Scotts Road
Tel: (65) 6738-0371
Fax: (65) 6738-3648

American Women's Association
21 Scotts Road
Tel: (65) 6733-6170
Fax: (65) 6733-6190

Australian & New Zealand Association (ANZA)
19 Tanglin Road #06-45
Tel: (65) 6733-1215
Fax: (65) 6735-9695

American Club
21 Scotts Road
Singapore 228219
Tel: (65) 6737-3411
Fax: (65) 6732-8308

British Club
73 Bukit Tinggi Road
Singapore 289761
Tel: (65) 6467-4311

Hollandse Club (Dutch Club)
22 Camden Park (off Adam Road)
Singapore 299814
Tel: (65) 6464-5225
Fax: (65) 6468-6272
Internet: www.hollandseclub.org.sg

Swiss Club
36 Swiss Club Road
Singapore 288139
Tel: (65) 6466-3233
Fax: (65) 6468-8550

German Club - Deutsches Haus
Farrer Road Post Office
P.O. Box 36
Singapore 912802
Tel: (65) 6463-1466
Fax: (65) 6463-3730

Tanglin Club
5 Stevens Road
Tel: (65) 6737-6011
Fax: (65) 6733-2391

Singapore Polo Club
80 Mt Pleasant Road
Tel: (65) 6256-4530
Fax: (65) 6256-6715

Belgium and Luxembourg Association of Singapore
Ulu Pandan Road
#16-406 BLK4 Pandan Valley
Singapore 597628
Tel: (65) 6469-2933
Internet: www.blas.org.sg
Email: secretary@blas.org.sg

British Association of Singapore
1 Selegie Road #08-26 Paradiz Centre
Tel: (65) 6339-8229
Fax: (65) 6339-1167

Canadian Association of Singapore
21 Scotts Road
Tel: (65) 6734-5954
Fax: (65) 6738-2726

Goethe Institut
163 Penang Road, #05-01 Winsland House II
Tel: (65) 6735-4555
Fax: (65) 6735-4666

Republic of Singapore Flying Club
Building 140 – B Picadilly
Seletar Air Base - East Camp
Singapore 797754
Internet: www.singaporeflyingclub.com

Singapore Club Aquanauts (Dive Club)
3 B Hyderabad Road
Singapore 119573
Website: www.sca.org.sg

Changi Sailing Club
32 Netheravon Road
Singapore 508508
Tel. (65) 6545-2876
Fax. (65) 6542-4235

Republic of Singapore Yacht Club
52 West Coast Ferry Road
Singapore 126887
Tel: (65) 6768-9288
Fax: (65) 6768-9280
Internet: www.rsyc.org.sg

Additional listings of social clubs in Singapore are available at: www.xpatxperience.com/lifestyle/singapore_clubs.shtml

■ TRAVEL

Transport & Travel in Singapore
Internet: http://tt.ecitizen.gov.sg/index.htm

Bus Information
Internet: www.sbstransit.com.sg

KTM Berhad
Internet: www.ktmb.com.my
Timetable and booking system for trains between Malaysia and Singapore

Land Transport Authority of Singapore (LTA)
Internet: www.lta.gov.sg
The LTA website provides information for all public transport systems, including the MRT and LRT rail systems.

Ministry of Transport
460 Alexandra Road #39-00 & #33-00 Storeys
PSA Building, Singapore 119963
Tel: (65) 6270-7988
Fax: (65) 6375-7734
Internet: www.mot.gov.sg
Email: mot@mot.gov.sg

■ SMRT
www.smrt.com.sg
SMRT website provides train and bus schedules

Changi Airport
Changi Airport Group (Singapore) Pte. Ltd
Singapore Changi Airport
PO Box 168
Singapore 918146
Tel: (65) 6595 6868
Internet: www.changiairport.com
The website provides flight information for all arrivals and departures at: www.changiairport.com.sg/changi/en/flight_information/arrival_departure/index.html#_test

■ AIRLINES

Singapore Airlines
Tel: (65) 6223-8888 (24 hours)
Internet: www.singaporeair.com

Tiger Airways
Internet: www.tigerairways.com

Silk Air
Tel: (65) 6223 8888 (24 Hours)
Internet: www.silkair.com

■ UNIVERSITIES

Nanyang Technological University (NTU)
50 Nanyang Avenue, Singapore 639798
Tel: (65) 67911744
Fax: (65) 67911604
Internet: www.ntu.edu.sg
Email: adm_intnl@ntu.edu.sg
NTU is a national university

National University of Singapore
21 Lower Kent Ridge Road, Singapore 119077
Tel: (65) 6516-6666
Fax: (65) 6778 3948
Internet: www.nus.edu.sg
Email: HR_Enquiry@nus.edu.sg

Singapore Management University (SMU)
Administration Building
81 Victoria Street
Singapore 188065
Tel: (65) 6828-0100
Fax: (65) 6828-0101
Internet: www.smu.edu.sg
Email: enquiry@smu.edu.sg
SMU is a national university

For additional listings of universities, refer to the Ministry of Education.

■ IMMIGRATION (VISAS)

Ministry of Foreign Affairs
Tanglin, Singapore 248163
Tel: (65) 6379-8000

Fax: (65) 6471-3901
Internet: www.mfa.gov.sg
Email: mfa@mfa.gov.sg
For information about visas, email: mfa_con@mfa.gov.sg

Singapore Information
Internet: www.entersingapore.info/sginfo/immigration.php

Immigration & Checkpoints Authority of Singapore
ICA Building
10 Kallang Road
Singapore 208718
Tel: (65) 6391-6100
Fax: (65) 6298-0837
Internet: www.ica.gov.sg

■ AIR CHECKPOINTS

Changi Airport
Internet: www.changiairport.com

Seletar Airport
Building 554 West Camp Road
Tel: (65) 6483-7003
Fax: (65) 6481-4504

■ LAND CHECKPOINTS

Tuas Checkpoint (24 Hours)
501 Jalan Ahmad Ibrahim

Woodlands Checkpoint (24 Hours)
21 Woodlands Crossing

COASTAL CHECKPOINTS

Singapore Cruise Centre (24 Hours)
HarbourFront Centre,
1 Maritime Square #01-18
Telok Blangah Road

Tanah Merah Ferry Terminal (0700hrs – 2300hrs)
50 Tanah Merah Ferry Road

Changi Point Ferry Terminal (0700hrs – 1900hrs)
51 Lorong Bekukong

Changi Ferry Terminal
30 Changi Ferry Road

Jurong Fishing Port (24 Hours)
Jurong Office, 35 Fishery Port Road

Marina South Pier (24 Hours)
31 Marina Coastal Drive

West Coast Pier (24 Hours)
60 West Coast Ferry Road

PORT CHECKPOINT

Ports Command HQ
Pasir Panjang Terminal Gate 4
33 Harbour Drive
Tel: (65) 6778-1193
Fax: (65) 6774-1109

■ WORKING IN SINGAPORE

Ministry of Manpower
18 Havelock Road
Singapore 059764
Tel: (65) 6438-5122
Internet: www.mom.gov.sg
Email: via website form

Foreign Manpower Management Division / Occupational Safety and Health Inspectorate
Ministry of Manpower
120 Kim Seng Road
Singapore 239436

Work Pass Services Centre (WPSC)
Tanjong Pagar Complex
7 Keppel Road #02-27/29
Singapore 089053

Employment Pass Services Centre (EPSC)
The Riverwalk
20 Upper Circular Road, #04-01/02
Singapore 058416

KEY FACTS FOR THAILAND

- **BUSINESS INVESTMENT**
Internet: www.boi.go.th

- **BUSINESS REGISTRATION**
Internet: www.moc.go.th; www.dbd.go.th
The Ministry of Commerce & The Department of Business Development

- **CLASSIFIED ADVERTISING**
Internet: www.bahtsold.com

- **CLIMATE**
Internet: www.tmd.go.th/en
Thai Meteorological Department

- **CURRENCY**
US$1.00 = 33.1898 THB (Thai Baht) on 9/2/10

- **EMBASSIES**
Internet: http://th.embassyinformation.com/

- **EMPLOYMENT**
Internet: www.doe.go.th
The Department of Employment issues work permits

- **FLIGHT INFORMATION**
Internet: www.aviation.go.th
Database of flight arrivals and departures

- **GOVERNMENT**
Internet: www.thaigov.go.th/eng/
Website of the Royal Thai Government

- **IMMIGRATION (VISAS)**
Internet: www.imm.police.go.th; www.immigration.go.th

- **INFORMATION**
Internet: www.thaivisa.com; www.thailand-uk.com
General information and forums for expats

JOBS FOR TEACHERS
Internet: www.ajarn.com; www.daveseslcafe.com

- **MINISTRY OF FOREIGN AFFAIRS**
Internet: www.mfa.go.th
Visa info: www.mfa.go.th/web/12.php
Consular and travel information for foreigners

- **RECRUITMENT**
Internet: www.jobthai.com; www.jobjob.co.th
Online recruitment databases

- **RETIREMENT IN THAILAND**
Internet: www.retiringinthailand.com
Guide book for retirees by Paiboon Publishing

- **THE BANGKOK POST**
Internet: www.bangkokpost.net
The primary English language newspaper of Thailand

- **TIME: GMT + 7 hours**

- **TOURISM AUTHORITY OF THAILAND**
Internet: www.tat.or.th
Tel: (66) 2250-5500

ADDITIONAL INFORMATION

- BUSINESS

Bank of Thailand
273 Samsen Road, Bangkhumprom
Bangkok 10200
Tel: (66) 2283-5353
Fax: (66) 2280-0449
Internet: www.bot.or.th

Board of Investment (BOI)
555 Vibhavadi-Rangsit Road,
Chatuchak, Bangkok 10900
Tel: (66) 2537-8111
Fax: (66) 2537-8177
Internet: www.boi.go.th
Email: head@boi.go.th
Business promotion and tax incentives for foreign industry to operate in Thailand. Further information is available at: www.investmentthailand.com (economic and commercial overviews including investment support policies for each province)

Board of Trade of Thailand
150/2 Ratchabophit Road, Bangkok 10200
Tel: (66) 2221-0555
Fax: (66) 2225-3995
Internet: www.tcc.or.th

Business Registration
Ministry of Commerce
Internet: www.deb.moc.go.th

Customs Department
Ministry of Finance
Atnarong Road, Klongtoey
Bangkok 10110
Tel: (66) 2249 0431
Internet: www.customs.go.th

Department of Business Development (DBD)
The Ministry of Commerce
Internet: www.dbd.go.th
The DBD website publishes the Thai laws

Department of Export Promotion
Ministry of Commerce
Tel: (66) 2513-1909
Fax: (66) 2512-1079
Internet: www.thaitrade.com; www.dep.moc.go.th

Department of Foreign Trade
Ministry of Commerce
Tel: (66) 2547-4771
Fax: (66) 2547 4791
Internet: www.dft.moc.go.th

Department of Industrial Promotion
Ministry of Industry
Tel: (66) 2202-4415
Fax: (66) 2246-0031
Internet: www.dip.go.th

Department of Land
Tel: (66) 2448-5448
Internet: www.dol.go.th
Valuation and registration of land in Thailand

General Post Office (GPO)
Tel: (66) 2233-1050
Internet: www.ptd.go.th
The GPO website displays international postal tariffs

Gold Traders
Internet: www.goldtraders.or.th
Market price for 1 Baht unit (weight) of gold

Industrial Estates Authority of Thailand
Ministry of Industry
Tel: (66) 2253-0561
Fax: (66) 2253-4086
Internet: www.ieat.go.th
Promotional incentives available

Investor Club Association (ICA)
TP & T Tower, 16th Floor, 1 Soi 19,
Vibhavadee Rangsit Road, Bangkok
Tel: (66) 2936-1429
Internet: www.ic.or.th
Email: investor@ic.or.th
ICA is a private members club, part of the Board of Investment (BOI), which serves as a networking organisation for BOI members. ICA Members have access to the Customs Department tracking system for raw materials and machinery.

Joint Foreign Chambers of Commerce in Thailand
Tel: (66) 2617-2075
Fax: (66) 2617-2089
Internet: www.jfcct.com
E-mail: fcccc@inet.co.th

Ministry of Commerce
44/100 Thanon Sanam Bin Nam-Nonthaburi
Muang District, Nonthaburi 11000
Tel: (66) 2507-8000
Fax: (66) 2547-5210
Internet: www.moc.go.th
Business and company registration

Ministry of Finance
Thanon Rama IV, Samsen-Nai,
Phayathai, Bangkok 10400
Tel: (66) 2273-9021
Fax: (66) 2293-9408
Internet: www.mof.go.th

Ministry of Industry
Rama IV Road, Ratchathewi, Bangkok 10400
Tel: (66) 2202-3000
Fax: (66) 2202-3048
Internet: www.moi.go.th

National Statistical Office
Internet: www.nso.go.th

Stock Exchange of Thailand (Set)
Internet: www.set.or.th

■ FRANCHISING

Franchise License Asia
Internet: www.franchiselicenseasia.com
Email: info@franchiselicenseasia.com
Franchise exhibitions and consulting

Horwath Franchise Services (Thailand) Limited
4th Floor, Thai CC Tower,
889 South Sathorn Road
Yannawa, Bangkok, 10120
Tel: (66) 2719-3515
Fax: (66 2719-3886
Internet: www.horwathap.com

Thailand Franchise Association
20/25 Seri Village
Soi Onnut, Sukhumvit 77
Bangkok 10250
Tel: (66) 2321-5129
Fax: (66) 2721-2795
Email: focus@bangkok.com

■ NEWSPAPERS & MAGAZINES

The Bangkok Post
Fax: (66) 2240 3664
Internet: www.bangkokpost.net
Email: business@bangkokpost.co.th
Classifieds: www.bangkokpostjobs.com

Citylife Magazine
Trisila Company Limited
3 Chom Doi Road, T. Suthep
Chiangmai 50200
Tel: (66) 5322-5201
Fax: (66) 5335-7491
www.chiangmainews.com
Email: info@chiangmaicitylife.com
Monthly magazine for expats of northern Thailand

Maplus Magazine
Bangkokstation Network Co., Ltd
33/125, 128 Wall Street Tower 25th Surawong Road
Suriyawong Bangrak, Bangkok 10500
Tel: (66) 2267-6178
Fax: (66) 2267-5539
Magazine for longstay foreigners (in both English & Japanese)

The Nation
44 Moo 10 Bang Na-Trat KM 4.5,
Bang Na district, Bangkok 10260
Tel: (66) 2325-5555
Fax: (66) 2751-4446
Internet: www.nationmultimedia.com
National English-language daily newspaper

Pattaya Mail
Pattaya Mail Publishing Co., Ltd
370/7-8 Pattaya Second Road,
Pattaya City, Chonburi 20260
Tel: (66) 3841-1240
Fax: (66) 3842-7596
Internet: www.pattayamail.com
E-mail: ptymail@loxinfo.co.th
Weekly English-language newspaper

■ SOCIAL CLUBS & NETWORKS

Bangkok Expats' Club
Internet: www.bangkok-expats-club.com

The British Club
Internet: www.britishclubbangkok.org

Chiangmai Expats' Club
Internet: www.chiangmaiexpatsclub.com
Email: info@chiangmaiexpatsclub.com
Meeting: 2nd and 4th Saturday of the month

European Young Professionals
Internet: www.europeanyoungprofessionals.org

Golf Clubs
Internet: www.golf-bangkok.com

International Business Association of Phuket
Internet: http://ibap-phuket.org
E-mail: info@ibap-phuket.org

The Foreign Correspondents' Club of Thailand (FCCT)
Penthouse, Maneeya Center
518/5 Ploenchit Road,
(BTS Skytrain: Chitlom Station)
Bangkok 10330
Tel: (66) 2652-0580
Internet: www.fccthai.com
Email: fccthai@loxinfo.co.th
FCCT is the social hub for media professionals in Bangkok.

■ TAXATION

Revenue Department
Phaholyothin, Soi 7, Bangkok 10400
Tel: (66) 2617-3000
Internet: www.rd.go.th
Revenue Code (tax law) and administration of taxes

■ TOURIST POLICE

Tourist Police
2170 Krungthep Tower Building, New Petchaburi Road
Bangkapi Huaykwang, Bangkok 10310
Tel: 1155
Internet: http://thaitouristpolice.com/main.php
Email: tourist@police.go.th
Tourist Police Division is agency affiliated with Central Investigation Bureau and Royal Thai Police, working under supervision of Ministry of Tourism and Sport. responsible for crime prevention and safety of tourists.

■ TRAVEL

Flight Information
Internet: www.aviation.go.th

Train Timetables
Internet: www.thailandbytrain.com

Tourism Authority of Thailand
Tel: (66) 2250-5500
Fax: (66) 2250-5511
Internet: www.tat.or.th; www.tourismthailand.org
Email: center@tat.or.th

■ WORK PERMITS

Department of Employment
Ministry of Labour & Social Welfare
Internet: www.doe.go.th
For work permit applications, refer to the website:
www.doe.go.th/service3_en.aspx

One-Stop Service Centre For Visas & Work Permits
Krisda Plaza 3rd Floor, 207 Rachadapisek Road,
Dindaeng, Bangkok 10310
Tel: (66) 2693-9333
Fax: (66) 2693-9352
Internet: www.boi.go.th
E-mail: visawork@boi.go.th
The centre can process visas and work permits in less than 3 hours.

KEY FACTS FOR VIETNAM

- BUSINESS
Internet: http://vibforum.vcci.com.vn;
www.amchamvietnam.com
Vietnam / American Chamber of Commerce & Industry

- CLASSIFIED ADVERTISING
Internet: www.expatvietnam.net
Free classified listings

- CURRENCY
1 US$ = 18429.8 VND (Vietnamese Dong) on 9 February 2010

- EMBASSIES
Internet: http://vn.embassyinformation.com

- EXPAT FORUMS
Internet: www.expatvietnam.net
Includes database of jobs in Vietnam

- GOVERNMENT
Internet: www.chinhphu.vn
Tel: (84) 4-804-3100
Government portal for Vietnam

- IMMIGRATION (VISAS)
Internet: www.vnimm.gov.vn
The Vietnam Immigration Department

- INFORMATION
Internet: www.livinginvietnam.com
Information for expats

- **MINISTRY OF EDUCATION & TRAINING**
Internet: www.moet.gov.vn
Tel: (84) 4-3869-5144
Accreditation of schools and universities in Vietnam

- **MINISTRY OF FINANCE**
Internet: www.mof.gov.vn

- **MINISTRY OF FOREIGN AFFAIRS (MOFA)**
Internet: www.mofa.gov.vn
MOFA provides consular and travel information

- **NEWSPAPER (VIETNAM NEWS)**
Internet: http://vietnamnews.vnagency.com.vn

- **NGO RESOURCE CENTRE**
Internet: www.ngocentre.org.vn
Website publishes NGO job listings

- **TIME: GMT + 7 hours**

- **TOURISM**
Internet: www.vietnamtourism.gov.vn
Vietnam National Administration of Tourism

- **VIETNAM INVESTMENT REVIEW**
Internet: www.vir.com.vn
Investment updates

- **WORK PERMITS**
Internet: www.business.gov.vn

GLOSSARY OF TERMS

Completion   *The final stage of business transfer when the Buyer legally owns the business*

Depreciation   *The hypothetical expense of using fixed assets. Usually fixed assets are amortised linearly over their estimated economic life*

Due Diligence   *The verification of information provided by the Seller to the Buyer*

Franchisee   *An independent business person who has been granted by the franchisor the right to duplicate its entire business format at a particular location and for a specified period, under terms and conditions set forth in the franchise agreement*

Freehold   *Legal ownership of the land or property*

Goodwill   *Goodwill is an intangible business asset, which includes the value of trademarks, contacts, future orders placed by customers, good location, specialist knowledge and business systems*

Net Book Value *The cost of a fixed Asset (eg equipment) less accumulated depreciation (to allow for wear and tear of the asset)*

Turnkey   *The business is fully operational and profitable from the date of transfer of business ownership to the Buyer*

ABOUT THE AUTHOR

Philip Wylie was born in Liverpool, UK. He has worked as Company Director, Business Manager, Company Secretary, Finance Manager, Interim Manager, Business Advisor, Tax Consultant, Sales Representative, Chief Accountant and Trainer for several SMEs and three top international companies in UK and the Middle East. He is a Fellow of The Institute of Chartered Accountants in England and Wales (FCA) and MBA (London).

As a undergraduate, Philip worked in USA as a camp counselor with the *Camp America* programme. *Camp America* enabled Philip to hitch hike across America and travel around Canada. Later Philip worked in the South of France as a plumber and electrician for an entrepreneur who rented mobile homes and caravans.

Since living in Southeast Asia, Philip has facilitated workshops in Hong Kong, Singapore and Malaysia, written books, and worked as a business broker and advisor with Sunbelt Asia in Thailand. All of the above adventures were created by Philip through NETWORKING. Philip lives with his Thai girlfriend, Bee, who teaches the art of cooking delicious Thai food.

FURTHER READING

We recommend books published by Paiboon Publishing (www.paiboonpublishing.com), particularly the language books; and books published by Fast Track Publishing (www.fasttrack-publishing.com).

How to Establish A Successful Business In Thailand, by Philip Wylie, published by Paiboon Publishing (www.paiboon-publishing.com) ISBN 978-1-887521-75-8

An indispensable bible for anyone thinking of starting or buying a small business in Thailand. Paiboon Publishing have produced the first real authority on the pitfalls and processes involved when setting up in Thailand, and a guide like this is likely to save many a naïve foreigner the rip-offs and failures that others before them have experienced. Now they have a useful reference on evaluating businesses, cutting through red tape, ownership restrictions, local business culture and essential contacts. Written by former business consultant Philip Wylie, the book lays out an easy step by step method to achieve the successes of some of the case studies mentioned in the book. A thorough and essential read.

- Bangkok 101 magazine

Email: fasttrackpublishing@gmail.com
Fax (Hong Kong): +852-3010-9769